Flash Nonfiction Food

91 Very Delicious, Very True, Very Short Stories

FLASH
Nonfiction
FOOD

91 Very Delicious,
VERY TRUE,
Very Short Stories

Edited by

Tom Hazuka *and* **Kathryn Fitzpatrick**

woodhall press
NORWALK, CONNECTICUT

Text and cover design by Casey Shain

Library of Congress Cataloging-in-Publication Data available
ISBN 978-1-949116-22-9

First Edition

Woodhall Press, 81 Old Saugatuck Road, Norwalk, CT 06855
WoodhallPress.com
Distributed by INGRAM

This is a book of flash nonfiction. Each author has created
a complete story in 750 words or fewer. Some pieces experiment
with form, others take a more traditional approach,
but all of them celebrate the precise and concise style of writing that
inspired Shakespeare to call brevity the soul of wit.

Preface

Let me start with a confession: I'm quite limited in the kitchen. As in, I hope you like tuna sandwiches or frozen pizza—or, on a good day, misshapen omelets. I truly enjoy eating, though, so I figure that makes me at least a semi-expert on food.

Flash Nonfiction Food wasn't even my idea: it was cooked up by the folks at Woodhall Press. It didn't seem like a half-baked project, and after editing other anthologies I knew I wouldn't be biting off more than I could chew. In fact, the project seemed to be my cup of tea, though I certainly didn't expect it to be as easy as pie. I enlisted my former student Kathryn Fitzpatrick as co-editor, figuring two cooks weren't sufficient to spoil the literary broth.

OK, I'll can the stomach-churning clichés before someone feeds me a knuckle sandwich.

Let's get cooking!

—TOM HAZUKA

When Dr. Hazuka asked me to join him as co-editor on Flash Nonfiction Food, there were two stipulations:

1. As a certified "young person," I'd be responsible for all social media promotion.

2. As co-editor, I'd call him Tom.

In all seriousness though, I could not be more excited about this book; I love food. (When I was twelve my parents had to block the Food Network on our cable box because I spent all day watching the Barefoot Contessa.)

Food speaks to our individual cultures, our histories, our social statuses, and our relationships. The essays in this book illustrate the foundational role food plays in our lives. There are stories about love and sickness and travel, and each shares a common thread in the sense that food brings it all together.

I hope you enjoy it as much as I do.

—KATHRYN FITZPATRICK

Table of Contents

B Is for Breakfast

ALICE LOWE

Bagels and lox were a rare treat during my childhood. Once or twice a year my family—New York transplants, nominal Jews acclimating to Southern California soil—indulged in a trip to the Bohemian Bakery in downtown San Diego. At home my father divided the scant half-pound of paper-thin salmon into four equal portions that we stretched over our cream cheese-covered bagels, like twin-size afghans on full-size beds. When my daughter and I celebrated our birthdays in New York last fall, we took our place in the line snaking out the door at Ess-A-Bagel on Third Avenue, reported to be Manhattan's best, for piled-high lox with cream cheese, onion and tomato oozing out the sides of a seedy, garlicky, everything bagel. My mother's spirit hovered over us.

Bittersweet scenes interrupt my reverie. I was thirty-two when my mother died, my father's call from the hospital a harsh blow in the faceless gloom of night. "I'm coming up," I said. "No," he told me, "wait until morning." Unable to sleep, I drove to their house before dawn. He sprang out the door as I pulled up. "Let's go get breakfast," he said. Not comfortable with displays of emotion, he must have figured I'd be more manageable in a public place. We sat across from each other in wooden near-silence at a twenty-four-hour Denny's. My pain was excruciating, muzzled grief fused with anger, even before I learned he'd already installed my mother's replacement.

Brunch on Mother's Day replaced at-home mornings when my daughter gave me handmade cards and gifts. After she acquired a husband and in-laws, Mother's Day became an ordeal: a waterfront restaurant, our two bound-in-marriage families crowded around a table amid a crowd of tables in a hot-house of perfumed and corsaged merriment. Mediocre food, rushed service, mimosas made with cheap sparkling wine. Now Mother's Day is a quiet one-to-one celebration with my daughter.

Bikers, surfers, and assorted beach dwellers—I was among the latter—gathered at Maynard's, a Pacific Beach institution, on Sunday mornings in the mid-'60s. New to legal drinking, if not to the sport itself, poor and hung over, young and invincible, we downed double orders of red beer and twenty-five-cent quasi-Spanish omelets.

Breaking up is hard to do before one's first cup of coffee. An ex-boyfriend often went to a rural diner for the pancakes. When the server said, "Hey guys—two days in a row!" I thought she'd confused us with someone else. Until I heard my guy's intake of breath, saw his grimace. I knew—at a gut level I'd always known—but betrayal before breakfast felt unnecessarily brutal.

Bacon-loving vegetarians are a cliché. During my first meatless incarnation in the '70s I craved bacon, dreamt about bacon, swooned when its smoky aroma wafted from a restaurant kitchen. Now my resolve teeters and falls as I reach across to my husband's plate. "Just a nibble," I say, glancing furtively over my shoulder like a shoplifter or adulterer as I nab a crispy-but-greasy morsel. My ecological, animal rights, and religious convictions are tenuous. Why deny myself?

Bread is universal and the mainstay of my morning. In Amsterdam I ate *brood* with *vlokken*—dark chocolate flakes on hot buttered toast. In Paris a flaky *pain au chocolat* with my *café au lait*. Toast in Italy was a ham-and-cheese sandwich, hot off the grill. English cookbook author Nigel Slater recalls in his memoir, *Toast: The Story of a Boy's Hunger*, "My mother burns the toast as surely as the sun rises each morning." But, "It is impossible not to love someone who makes toast for you." It's reciprocal. My mother's toast, with margarine, cinnamon, and sugar, was love incarnate.

Books and stories serve breakfast as morning meal or metaphor, from Homer's *Odyssey* to James Joyce's *Ulysses*. In *The Hobbit*, Gandalf consumes, "[t]wo whole loaves with masses of butter and honey and clotted cream." Anthony Trollope's cleric in *The Warden* enjoys "eggs in napkins, and crispy bits of bacon under silver covers, and little fishes in a little box, and devilled kidneys frizzling on a hot-water dish." "Breakfast" is a story by John Steinbeck, a chapter of *Moby Dick*, martinis in *Breakfast of Champions*, a symbolic escape in *Breakfast at Tiffany's*.

Breaking the fast means so much more, like burnt toast or the sound and smell of sizzling bacon. Lox and bagels, brunches and betrayals. Breakfast renders the past palpable, grounds the present, portends the future. ◆

Hardly Any Food at All

KIM ADDONIZIO

Our instructor showed us the enema kit. He talked about the program: a week of lymphatic exercises in the mornings, then lectures on nutrition, a two-day liquid fast involving Rejuvelac and wheatgrass juice, and meals of healthy food (which I would soon learn meant hardly any food at all). Massage and colonics were available, and cost extra. We had paid to be on a starvation diet because of what our instructor called a "health challenge;" my boyfriend hadn't managed to quit smoking, and I'd convinced him to try this. It was day one and already we were miserable. He was freaking out without nicotine and I was repelled by the whole setup, which required faux intimacy with health-challenged strangers. Also, though religion wasn't mentioned in the brochure I'd skimmed, we'd been asked earlier to visualize "the Creator," each according to our faith (I have none: God is a fairy tale; life is meaningless; get over it).

We'd all had to hold hands in a big circle after the first slide presentation and lecture. Fun facts: Elvis's body, when he died, was filled with sixty pounds of impacted fecal matter. The average woman eats four pounds of lipstick in her lifetime. Carbonated anything is a bad idea. Alcohol damages the nerves, kills brain cells, and increases the risk of breast cancer. In the slide show, the healthy cells readying their attack on a cancer cell resembled fuzzy blue tennis balls. The cancer cell had some kind of netting over it, like a small brown animal trapped in the jungle. The good cells bored holes in the cancer cell and destroyed it until only the netting was left. After the presentation, we were asked to hug our neighbors. I hugged my boyfriend and dragged him away before anyone could get close.

We filed into the dining room for lunch, artfully plated on orange plastic, and sat down to mung beans, dandelion greens, buckwheat greens, and alfalfa sprouts. A tiny mound that possibly aspired to be falafel—mushy and brown, possibly a dying cancer cell—squatted in the center. It tasted the way I imagine wood pulp might. I immediately wished for prime rib and several whiskey-and-Cokes to wash it down, imagining a court full of blue tennis balls being lobbed, one by one, high above the baseline and over the fence.

After lunch, our group of twenty or so stood around a table that held a flat of wheatgrass, a large silver juicer, and several bowls. Wheatgrass is crude chlorophyll. It can, reportedly, detoxify the body, regulate blood sugar, and promote weight loss. It has vitamins and antioxidants. The benefits sound appealing, until you actually taste it. We each took a bowl to the glassed-in refrigerator for some grass, rinsed it at the sink, then turned to a row of smaller juicers. We juiced two ounces to drink, and another four to put up our tushes (our instructor's word) for our self-administered enemas that evening. First, the water enema—hold it up in your tush for five minutes—followed by the wheatgrass one—hold for twenty minutes while massaging your colon. (Your colon will be the thing inside you that is cramping badly.) What didn't get juiced writhed slowly out the front of my machine, like a verdant turd from a tush, a green clot of wrung-out grass. This can be used as a poultice to soothe a sunburn or poison ivy rash. You can chew it to cure bad breath. You can stick it in your ears to pull out earwax.

If, like me, you have ever been foolish enough to try a wheatgrass enema, you will never want to smell the stuff, let alone taste it, again.

On the third day, my boyfriend and I rose lightheaded from the near-death of near-starvation and fled back to the toxic world, forfeiting most of the money we'd paid. On the way home, we stopped at a motel for the night. We conjured an unholy feast from the vending machines—Pringles, BBQ Doritos, M&M's, Snickers bars, cans of Dr. Pepper and Pepsi. The girl at the reception desk had bad skin and I would bet you a high colonic she had never drunk liquid grass or put it up her ass. My boyfriend bummed a couple of Marlboro Lights from her. As far as I know, he never did quit smoking. Wherever he is now, I apologize for everything I did to him while we were together, and I wish him good health. ◆

Hospitality

SHAHNAZ HABIB

is when she walks into your restaurant, a tired young woman in fading clothes, because it is the only one that is still open past midnight on Atlantic Avenue and orders the cheapest thing on the menu and then she starts scrambling to put together three dollars for a falafel sandwich from the dimes and quarters in her wallet, and she asks about the shakshuka, do you make it only for breakfast, and you sense that this is what she would really like on this weary night, and you tell her, you want the shakshuka? no problem, and she says no, no, I was just asking, but you tell her it's okay, you don't mind, and you wave away the rest of the money though the shakshuka is not the cheapest thing on the menu and then like a priest, you bring out warm grilled bread and a fierce bubbling shakshuka, a blessing on this cold Brooklyn night, and you watch her eat and at first both of you are polite but soon you cannot resist, where are you from, yes, I thought so, India or Pakistan, somewhere in that direction, and you tell her you are from Djibouti and you can see from her expression though it hasn't changed that she does not have the vaguest idea where it is but doesn't want to offend you by asking, so without missing a beat you tell her that Djibouti is across the Red Sea from Yemen, that you have often taken that ten-minute boat to Yemen to go shopping and that is why you are here serving Yemeni food in a Yemeni restaurant in Brooklyn though you are from another country, but you really aren't because you can walk their walk, talk their talk, but you really are because you are also African, and Somalia and Ethiopia and Eritrea flank you protectively, a little too protectively, you see, Djibouti, you tell her, is like the Kashmir of North Africa, but it is okay, you don't mind, it's all good and now you pour her and you a cup of mint tea and sit at her table and she drops a word into the conversation that you seize with impatience, your eyes glistening in the glare of the harsh overhead light, and the word is colonialism and now you do not have enough time to tell her everything, you tell her about studying in Paris and you imitate the cop with the frozen voice at the corner of every street asking you for your ID, how you learnt, early and automatically, to go all over the world and live in every corner as if you were invisible but to return to Djibouti where nobody worries you, Djibouti where Africa meets the Arab world, how one day you will go back to Djibouti which sailors many centuries ago called the Land of Welcoming, and you tell her, you must come to my country, you must come someday, it is a beautiful country with beautiful people, and that is hospitality. ◆

Blood Oranges

DALLAS CROW

If I painted, I would have a blood orange period to rival Picasso's blue period. I'd spend years teasing out the infinite variety of their marbled blushings, these enchanted orbs illuminated from within by some mysterious dark radiance. Still lifes, of course, but also landscapes with the oranges foregrounded so they are more prominent than mountains or ocean, echoing the setting sun on one canvas, the full moon rising on another. Abstract explosions of purple and orange. If some modern Medici paid me enough, I'd paint him—nearly eclipsed by the ravishing fruit glowing in the palm of his hand. ◆

Mayonnaise and Apricot Jam

JENNY KLION

My mom once made me write a list of my ten favorite foods, and I couldn't come up with enough entries, so I put down "salt" as number ten. The others were apple, peanut butter, peanut butter sandwich, French fries, pizza, hot dog, cookies, iceberg lettuce, French toast—not with syrup, I did not like syrup—and salt.

Never mind my mom munched on mayonnaise and apricot jam sandwiches, I can assure you I eat neither of these foods, and don't allow mayonnaise in my house. I felt a bit guilty about this no-mayo policy when my daughter was growing up, but not enough to change it. I'm flexible about many things; regarding mayonnaise, no.

My grandmother Henrietta, my dad's mom, was apparently a genius chef of the Jewish variety, yet I really have no idea, because I wanted nothing to do with her carrot-and-cucumber marinades, or chopped chicken livers, or whatever kind of smoked fish fancies my family was always drooling over. I did love her roasted potatoes, crisped on the outside, dripping with lard or chicken fat probably, creamy deliciousness on the inside. And I'd dip them in salt.

The picky eating was a sore spot for me. I took a lot of flak for that Skippy peanut butter jar I clung to on a family vacation—all the way to Paris and back again.

I was seven years old, and the trip did not cure my fussiness, though I liked French sugar crepes and also ham sandwiches, but totally plain, with no butter or cornichons.

My parents did not force me to eat anything, save for one time when there was a snafu at the dinner table, and suddenly I was sitting alone in front of a portion of brussels sprouts I refused to touch. Ironic in retrospect, because I doubt my mom ate hers either. She usually subscribed to a dinner of "dry chicken with rosemary"—her words, not mine—along with iceberg lettuce, Good Seasons salad dressing, and rolls. She did not like vegetables, up to the end.

That night of the brussels sprouts drama I remained in my seat steadfastly, staring at a plate that looked the antithesis of Henrietta's roasted potatoes. Here was a similarly small, round vegetable, except it was green, and hard, and ugly and dry, not to mention cold, and there was no way I would try it, not even with salt.

I could hear my mom doing dishes in the kitchen, I could hear my dad stomping around the den, and I could sense my two older sisters upstairs somewhere, looking down at me, wondering if I was going to crack. I didn't.

Sometime later the plate was removed, untouched, and I was punished. No TV for a week. I sobbed on the way back to my room—oh, the indignity of it all—though I got my sentence cut short and was back to watching *Batman* or *Bewitched* soon after.

If you offered me brussels sprouts now, I'd probably say yes, if properly prepared to my liking! I'm still picky about some things—hello, mayonnaise—but I have expanded my food repertoire, and don't use much salt anymore either. In fact, Henrietta taught me how to bake, and I have her prize-winning recipes for Brownie Pie and Broiled Coffee Cake. I miss her fancy apartment on the Upper West Side, with the long hallways we'd run up and down and get splinters on, and her roasted potatoes dripping with fat, which my sisters and cousins and I still moon over.

When my mom was dying, not long ago, she began to eat less and less. I tried tempting her with lots of comfort foods, like my own roast potatoes, or cheese toasts, or chicken rice soup, but she wouldn't have much. I gave her snack foods like Goldfish, or mini cookies I'd bake, or tea sandwiches that included her favorite apricot jam, but of course no mayonnaise, and definitely no brussels sprouts. She might've nibbled some of that. Mostly she didn't. In the end it didn't matter, because forget about picky, she stopped eating altogether.

My daughter tattooed a miniature orange apricot on the inside of her upper arm, in honor of my mom, who died before she could see it. I like the way the juicy fruit changes shape, depending on how my daughter moves, or from some angles you can hardly notice it at all. Thankfully, she is a very good eater. ◆

Butchering

JEFF NEWBERRY

i.

"Butcher" has nearly disappeared from public use. Customers prefer "meat cutter" because they associate "butcher" with "slaughter," and therefore "cruelty." My father was not a certified butcher. He learned the trade working with his brother in grocery stores when they were young. My father's job consisted of cutting steaks and grinding hamburger meat and running the band saw through thick beef slabs. He'd lay out the freshly cut chops into sterilized Styrofoam trays, each cut with a plastic pad beneath it to soak up any runoff from the meat. He often cut himself—his hand, his knuckles. He went to work in sanitized white and came home, smock stained red. You couldn't tell where his blood ended, where the animal's began.

ii.

"Butcher" is a synonym for "murder" or "slaughter." You can hear it on the news after a gruesome attack: "Man butchers three at local Walmart." You can read it in history books about regimes who "butchered" populations. We use "butcher" to talk about language, how certain people "butcher" a phrase. Each time I hear it, I have to listen again. For me, the butcher is the man in white, the one who cuts the once-living into neat rows of steaks and chops for us to consume. Perhaps there is a connection here? Perhaps "butcher" means to do the things we can never face doing on our own. "I really butchered that one," I heard a musician say once after a botched song. Everyone agreed.

iii.

Cut this section. Cut that one. Cut it out. Carve out some time. Slice of life vignette. Our language is filled with images of butchering. I tell students to "cut your prose down. Move your subjects and verbs closer together. Cut the fat," as though language were meat, as though behind these lines of neat words, it exists as an animal might, grazing in my brain, wild and free.

Someone had to kill it. Someone had to bring the carcass to the butcher who, with practiced hands, cut and carved until only what matters remains. Like Michelangelo before a stone, I sometimes think the story exists buried in language. I forget that before I take up my knife, I have to invent the creature who roams the woods alone. ◆

You've Been Chopped!

SARAH WESLEY LEMIRE

When it comes to guilty pleasures, mine include listening to Air Supply's "All Out of Love," consuming an entire canister of Moose Munch popcorn in a single sitting, and binge-watching *Chopped*. In a perfect world, it's some combination of all three with a bottle of chardonnay in arm's reach.

Chopped has long been a favorite of mine. I love the moment when host Ted Allen dramatically lifts the cover off the loser's dish and sighs, "Chef Blah Blah, you'vvveee been chooopppppeeed," in a single, long, drawn-out, breath.

I also like the judges. Tough-but-fair Alex Guarnaschelli, the red onion-and-overcooked pasta-hating Scott Conant, and saucy Aarón Sánchez, who always pronounces Latino foods with a heavily accented flair and roll of his tongue, making ingredients like taco chips baked from minced grasshoppers sound like something I actually might want to eat.

Sometimes I think I could be a contestant. I've had a lot of experience. In fact, Food Network could swing by my house on any given night and shoot an episode with little to no advance warning.

Too lazy to hit the grocery store and almost always out of food, I frequently cook dinner using only what I have on hand. This usually includes some kind of freezer-burned meat, a can of pumpkin expired in a different calendar year, and a pencil sharpener.

Similar to the show, I often end up with a catastrophic injury, like the time I invested in a porcelain paring knife that was sharper than a French Revolution guillotine. The very first time I used the knife, I sliced open a finger attempting to chop garlic. Serious enough to require gauze and medical tape, I dressed the wound and returned to the task.

Apparently having learned nothing at all from the experience, I immediately did it again, almost severing a finger off the good hand, leaving me with two heavily-bandaged pointers, and shutting down production for the rest of the night.

As on *Chopped*, the judges at my house are a tough crowd.

My husband: on a required low salt, low sugar diet. My elder daughter: a vegetarian. And my younger daughter: a medically diagnosed supertaster.

Supertasters, for the uninitiated, have exponentially more taste buds than ordinary people, making many foods too pungent, bitter, or sweet. In other words, it's statistically impossible to cook anything they will eat outside of plain pasta and frozen Eggo waffles.

Working under those conditions, the only thing I routinely put on the table that everyone agrees on is silverware.

Like most contestants, I have a compelling backstory. When I was growing up, my mom, who thankfully is still around and will hotly debate me on this, didn't like to cook. Oh sure, she made us a lot of wonderful meals. But there were also plenty of nights where she'd take out all the pans and set them on the stove, indicating that at some point she planned on cooking something in them.

Instead, they'd sit empty for a couple of hours before she'd default to Stouffer's Chicken Tetrazzini heated up in the microwave.

In similar fashion, she also liked to set the vacuum cleaner in the middle of the room if we were expecting company, implying that they'd interrupted her just as she was preparing to go on a vacuum bender, even if it was the farthest thing from the truth.

When my mom did cook, everything was "gourmet."

If we ate our salad after dinner, it was because that's how the "gourmets" did it. If we used frozen orange juice in our Minute Rice, it was because that's how the "gourmets" ate it. If dessert consisted of a banana set into a pineapple ring, topped with Miracle Whip and a cherry, that was gourmet, too.

And because we lived twenty miles from the nearest grocery store, we rarely, if ever, had all the ingredients for any given recipe, which meant that nearly every meal included at least one inspired substitution.

An optimist, my mom believed that it was perfectly acceptable to swap one ingredient for another, as long as they both fell into the same general food group, especially when it came to dairy products.

Sour cream worked for whipped cream on top of gingerbread. Skim milk was a stand-in for Cool Whip, because who doesn't like that on top of sliced bananas? And since cottage cheese sounded a lot like ricotta cheese, they were virtually interchangeable.

When I think about it, my mom would have been the perfect contestant on *Chopped*. With all her gourmet dishes and creative improvising, she'd have won. ◆

When Food Becomes Love

JO VARNISH

I sat with my dad, tucked up in his bed in England, the crisp sheets smoothed over his ironed pajamas. I'd made him dinner: pie, mash, and liquor— a substitute for the eels, pie, mash and liquor we had planned to eat in London's Shepherd's Bush before his illness made it impossible. The smell of the warm pastry filled the room. I had bought the ingredients—thankfully the shop nearby didn't have jellied eel—and prepared it his way. "The pie *must* be upside down," he'd often said as I was growing up. So it was: an upside-down pie of ground meat in a golden flaky pastry crust and a mound of mashed potatoes, smooth and creamy. A lake of green liquor, comprising parsley and fish stock, completed the dish.

My dad was, in English terms, a *grafter*. He rode his bike to work the Saturday after he left school at age fifteen, working six and a half days a week for a coach-building firm. After a few years, he and his brother moved out of London and started out on their own. Kumarlo Body Works was born, and for the next thirty years, Dad worked stressful weekdays, and then toiled long weekend days on the land he bought as his business grew. Putting up and maintaining fences, chopping wood for the winter, repairing his tractors, mowing his lawns. Life on five acres in a semi-rural location was a far cry from his government housed childhood; none of the local restaurants served his favorite childhood dish and he never stopped craving the tastes from his past.

Dad loved family and food, preferably together. Eating was integral to his enjoyment of life, and he was known for his voracious appetite. On leaving a restaurant, if he didn't feel "stuffed," he felt it a waste. He once enjoyed a three-course meal with a friend, and as they finished their desserts, they decided they weren't ready to leave. To the amusement of the waiter, they started again, ordered a further three courses, and finished every bite.

As a child, my father regaled us with his love of eels, pie, mash, and liquor, but it wasn't clear to me that this was a dish that actually consisted of real eels. "Eelspiemashanlicker" was a long set of syllables. I didn't consider the eels part until my brother Daniel bought my dad some from the Harrods Food Hall when I was twelve. A pot of jellied eels, far fancier than Dad was used to from the East End pie shops of his youth, was a rare treat for him that I couldn't bring myself to taste.

As Dad lay beside me, I reminded him of a trip that he, Daniel, my husband Jase, and I had taken a couple of years before. We drove him around London. We visited one of his homes, bombed in the war as he, his brother, and parents hid in the underground station. We saw the hatch in the side of a church where Dad and the other street kids lined up to be passed fresh bread by the nuns. We saw the areas he and his friends would search for shrapnel to play with during the war. For lunch, we went for eels, pie, mash and liquor.

Now, my version of that meal sat steaming on the table beside us. Dad's taste buds had betrayed him months before, a symptom of his kidney cancer, or a cruel side effect of its treatment. To Dad's distress, my stepmother's legendary meals of shepherd's pie, roast lamb, and grilled fish were rendered bland to his diminished palate.

"What have you done differently?" he asked her.

"Nothing," she replied, eyes glistening.

Feeding Dad was no longer about providing him with the tastes of his past lives, bringing forth vivid memories triggered by an herb, a spice, a flavor. Instead, this meal, just thirteen days before he passed away, was about showing him I cared. By eating it, he showed me the same. Preparing this dish, pie upside down, was an act of love, and my dad accepted it as such.

"It's really nice, Sweetheart," he whispered in between spoonfuls. ◆

Four Menus

SHEILA SQUILLANTE

1.

We're eating Korean soup tonight. *Yook gae jang*—shredded beef with cellophane noodles, scallions, and some long, fibrous, mysterious vegetable. And spice—mouthfuls of red oil that make my nose run and my tongue sing. I am in love with the man across the table whose nose is running too. We glisten and are happy. Happiness is the long tails of soybeans slicked with sesame oil, the strings hanging from our mouths. We sip soup and poke at condiments with our wooden chopsticks—the kind that snap and splinter, but who cares? I skewer a piece of jellied fish cake; bring it quivering to his lips. Another new, unexpected texture. When we eat together for the first time, it is before knowledge. Before the waitress knows our spice preferences: his flaming; mine not meek but milder. Before she has suggested other menu items (*Dol sot bibimbap* crisping in hot Korean crockware) and even steered us clear of some (codfish soup—bland, no depth, not good). All before we know where our tastes will take us. I am a self-proclaimed gourmand, having tried everything offered me at least once, but I have never before this night eaten the Korean pickled cabbage called kimchi. I know nothing of the way its slight carbonation will incite, the way its crunch will satisfy. It's a revelation, that first bite. I feel extended; I surpass myself. The whole room ferments! Poetry! Kimchi! Philosophy! Later, when we sit kissing on my second-hand couch, he will exclaim, "I love your eyebrows!" and I will touch them and fall.

2.

Food is love. Samuel Butler said, "Eating is touch carried to the bitter end." I understand. I was in Paris with friends. We sat in a park where parents played with their children, bundled in colorful wools for the early March chill. They kicked yellow balls, ran laughing after each other, their hoods flapping behind them. "I want to eat them!" I exclaimed. I am 32 years old and childless. I am childless and in love with a man who's not sure he wants children. Some days I crave. I am a lean witch cackling hungrily into a bone-cold wind.

3.

In my twenties, I was voted "Most Succulent" among my closest friends. We had just seen a film in which plane crash survivors must resort to cannibalism among the wreckage and the snow. After, it was decided that my ample fig-ure paired with my high energy would make for the tastiest meat. We made a pact: "If we ever crash on top of a snow-topped mountain and I die, you have my blessing to eat me." *Blessing*: an invocation of good fortune. If we crash and I die, I hope they are blessed with the warmth of a fire and time for slow cooking, for dining with relish and reverence, knowing that my spirit hovers, toasting their survival.

4.

For some, food is an inconvenience, something that wastes time. No. Food *extends* time, slows it for us generously. I cook because I believe in a slow life, a life of praise. I cook for my friends because I see them as divine. I cook to make holy moments, to call out and to reflect. I cook complex recipes in atonement. I gave up religion long ago. Now Sundays are for another kind of supper—one that acknowledges the sacrifices of human relationships. Sundays are for mundane tomato sauce stirred through with thyme and oreg-ano and worship for the sensual world. It's a kind of worship that makes it impossible to ignore the implication of the body, the way food changes us, fills us with our own good, hearty love. Food is worship, and God, to me, is kimchi, kalamata olives, artichoke hearts, and roasted garlic popped hot from its skin and spread warm with butter on bakery bread. God is lamb shanks braised long in orange juice and cabernet; is chopping Spanish onions with a heavy knife; is bittersweet chocolate chunked from dark Swiss bars. Is bittersweet entirely. ◆

Fire and Pie

ROBERT POPE

The town was Berkeley, the year 1967. Every day I passed a bakery on Telegraph with strawberry pie in the window, basket-weave crust over huge strawberries in thick glaze. It arrived each morning like an epiphany, smell and sight real, the taste imaginary. Nothing else existed for five minutes of each morning, not John Milton, not Descartes: *Volo ergo sum.* Once past the bakery I returned to the appropriate place in my journey, book bag on my shoulder, until the day I found five dollars on the sidewalk, slapped the bill on glass, and gave a serious woman in a white apron the truest sentence I knew: "I want that pie."

Heading back to my apartment, the bottom floor of a house three blocks down Dwight, I stopped for red wine with the change—five dollars went that far. When I walked into the apartment, Vicky looked up from the couch, where she sat smoking and reading. "What brings you home so soon?"

I slipped my book bag—wine inside—onto the floor, the white box behind my back, and shut the door with my foot. She was a short woman with a native look; long, straight golden-brown hair, in a turtleneck and corduroys thin at the ass. I opened the box before her narrowed eyes.

"What'd you do, steal it, for God's sake?"

In a few minutes we had crowded in the tight quarters of the kitchen with our friend Susan, at a rickety Formica table, pie glowing in the light of a candle stuck in the neck of a Chianti bottle. We pulled a thin yellow paisley curtain across the kitchen entrance to heighten an illusion of privacy and ritual. I cut three wedges, set them on individual cracked plates, and poured three jelly glasses of wine.

The only music was our happy groans before a pounding at the door made us pause, forks in the air. I became alarmed when I heard wood splintering, but nothing broke the spell of wine and pie until an enormous fireman in black slicker and helmet pushed aside the curtain with an ax.

We stared in silence until Susan said, "Would you like some pie?"

"Your house is on fire," he said. "Take what you need and get out."

When he left I shoved my typewriter in its case and tossed manuscripts and books in a cardboard box. Vicky grabbed clothes and Susan carried pie and wine.

A fire truck throbbed in the street, the fireman on the ladder flooding water from a tumid hose into the attic, where flames of red and yellow shot forth like snakes from Medusa's head. Several more worked at the house, and clumps of chance students stood about discursively as we fled across the street to set up camp. Susan set the pie and wine on the box, and we sat down and finished it while the house burned down. I remember no regrets, only the good taste of fire and pie. ◆

Lunches with Louie

DIANE GOODMAN

Sometimes people interpret silence as indifference, dismissiveness, even purposeful meanness. My grandfather was probably misunderstood as a nasty man because he didn't like to talk. When he did, he was a man of few words who, like the teenage me, was more comfortable communicating in gestures.

In high school I hung out with the irreverent kids at a hole-in-the-wall called, of all things, the Confectionary. We drank Coke for breakfast, fed the jukebox, played pool, cut classes, and made up lies for our absences that were taken for truth because school administrators were too busy with 3,000 students to check. Our parents were not very involved in our lives and there seemed to be an accepted code that while we might be seen from time to time, generally we should not be heard. This worked for us. When rare attempts were made to force us into talking, we reverted to angsty silence, the quick smirk, the eye roll, the listless shrug. We were, for better or worse, annoyed mimes.

On the first Monday of every month during high school, I met my grandfather Louie at a place across the street that made the absolute greatest cheeseburgers in the universe: Mawby's. Looking back, I imagine this was the day he received a check from somewhere. If you know anyone who lived on the east side of Cleveland, Ohio, in that era, they will wax poetic about the burgers at Mawby's. Skinny, nearly-crumbling patties flash fried on that dark, shiny griddle, the intoxicating smell that absorbed into your clothes the second you opened the door, the warm squishy bun, the grilled onions— crispy and caramelized before anyone used that word—salty-sweet. I'm sure there were fries and shakes and other items on the menu but I only remember the burgers.

He would be sitting at the counter when I got there, sipping black coffee. The Coke he had ordered for me when he arrived was already getting watery from the ice melting, the glass would be sweating, and when I slid onto the stool, he'd push it toward me. I'd take a sip, nod, and give him a kiss on his rough, stubbly cheek. Even if Louie and I had wanted to talk, we wouldn't have been able to hear each other over the noisy crowd also seated at the counter and the row of people standing behind, anxiously waiting for someone to finish and leave. You didn't go to Mawby's to have a leisurely lunch or to catch up with friends: you went there to eat the cheeseburgers.

The grill cooks were also the waiters. The one closest to us would turn around and say, "Cheeseburgers?" and I would raise four fingers, so Louie and I could each have two. "Onions?" A nod. Then we would sit there watching the burgers being salted and peppered and flipped—just once—and pressed so hard into the flattop that tiny golden droplets of meaty oil would fly up like miniature fireworks, then settle on top of the thick American cheese slice that had just been applied.

When our burgers came, the steam from the buns was a full-on facial, deeply redolent of the miracle mix of grease, grilled meat, still-melting cheese, and onions fried just this side of burnt. In unison, we lifted our first one and bit in. Heaven. Midway through the second, Grandpa Louie would nudge me with his elbow and I'd nod—tacit agreement that these were the best things to eat on earth—and we'd keep on eating. The burgers were soft and small and so delicious that, like most truly blissful things, the whole experience was over almost as soon as it began. In ten minutes, we were done. Then we'd both down our drinks, wipe our mouths, and barely stand before the people waiting behind us edged themselves onto our stools. Louie would put a ten dollar bill on the counter, which was way more than our lunch cost, and with his hand on my shoulder, I'd lead us through the crowd to the door.

When we got outside, he'd put his hand in his pocket because he always brought me something. A wide-mouthed pink comb, a pack of Juicy Fruit gum, once three cats' eye marbles, once a Bic pen. Somehow, he knew how much I needed these things, which I held tightly in a balled fist deep in my jacket pocket on my way back to the Confectionary. ◆

Of Samosas Stale and Fresh

LAKSHMI IYER

A plate of samosas sits in front of me. Steam coils in wisps above the coffee cup, dissipating into nothingness. Nursery rhymes play in a loop on my phone. Sahana hums along as she drinks her milk. I pick one of the samosas and feel for a moment how limp it is. I tear a piece and pop it into my mouth. An intense longing for the crispy onion-and-potato-filled samosas of my childhood in Madras overpowers me. I can taste the raw onion chutney, pungent, sharp, and exploding with flavors in my mouth. I feel disoriented. I pull myself together and get through the ritual of my evening coffee before the kids get home.

I realize with a start that this month will mark seventeen years of my moving to this country. I remember days when such longing would have caused me to drag Kannan out and drive over two hundred miles for fresh samosas and chaat. I sigh and promise myself that I will not eat limp samosas no matter how tempting they may seem. At least I will attempt to heat them in the oven instead of the microwave. It occurs to me that this mindset, right here, is probably a legacy of being an immigrant.

The making do, the approximating, the substituting, and the attitude of settling for somewhat similar. I lean back as I watch Sahana clap her hands in glee and realize the moringa leaves in the fridge will not be tinged with emotion for her as they do for me. All around me are marks of a person in flux. As I look ahead to our summer in India, I realize the lens through which I view India is not the same lens my daughters will see through. For them, it is an adventure. For me it is a pilgrimage.

I am tempted to pull out my wedding albums, to trace my fingers along the younger me as if to figure out if there are physical repercussions of being transplanted in alien soil. Then I realize I pass it each day in the mirror, in my closet full of clothes, in my kitchen pantry. The etchings that come from battling the dichotomy. In the long-distance calls that mark my mornings. In the token celebrations over the weekend of every major festival. The colors that seem faded and the sweets that seem tame. The LED lights replacing the thick smell of oil lamps. The ready-made rangolis that decorate my golu, the silver coconut and mango leaves that stand in for the real deal.

I see it in the six large suitcases in the under-the-stairs closet. I see it in gilded picture frames that grace the back of my study shelf. I see it in the avocado parathas and the coconut garnish on daikon cubed and curried.

The melding of selves, old and new; the faint longing for a life lived in a different universe and the gratitude for the life I currently live. I reach for the second bite of my now cool and limp samosa and savor it slowly, knowing this is better than no samosa. ◆

How to Be Poor

TAMARA GANE

Pancakes are acceptable for dinner if that's all they gave you the makings for at the food bank. If you also received a can of peaches or a jar of peanut butter, use one of them for a topping and convince your son it's not food for poor people but a fun game called *Breakfast for Dinner.*

If he hands you a note stating you need to send him to school tomorrow with $6.00 for a field trip, don't yell at him for not giving it to you sooner. Instead, wait until he goes to bed and gather change from underneath the couch cushions and on top of the washing machine. Run out to the car to check the console and between the seats. Count it. Put the $4.27 in an envelope with a note saying it's all you have and to please not say anything to your son because it will embarrass him. Seal the envelope before you put it in his backpack. Tell him to give it to his teacher without reading it. Try not to cry when he heads out the door.

Expect to be pulled over frequently by the police no matter how carefully you adhere to the law because you drive an old, beat-up car. They will speak to you sternly and ask if you have drugs. They will look at you like you're not a real person.

Learn to lie so you can tell your son you're not hungry on nights when there isn't enough food for two. Live with the shame of your circumstances, knowing this is all your fault. Feel you deserve this life so deeply it hurts your bones.

But also know this. Poverty does not define you. You devour books at night. You see things, understand things. Your inner thoughts run deep and wide. You have value, even if no one else sees it. Even if you don't see it yourself.

Someday you will take all those words in your head and put them down on paper. Poems will burst from your fingers like flames. Remember this as you peer inside your empty refrigerator.

You have flour, water, potatoes, and a cube of chicken bouillon. It's enough to make soup for dinner. You carry the bowls to the table, steaming and hot. Your son says it's delicious. And words fall down like rain. ◆

Weed Eaters

DINTY W. MOORE

My neighbor, a god-fearing, fastidious woman in her late sixties, spends hours on her hands and knees prying dandelions out of her lawn, eradicating any trace of the stubborn weed that sprouts rough yellow flowers and destroys the green symmetry of the planted carpet fronting her home. My usual reaction when I catch a glimpse out the window is to wince, because her knees are a dozen or so years more ancient than mine, and frankly, all of that kneeling has to hurt.

Sarah grew up on a farm, and she has kept that rural work ethic, despite the fact that her small city lot is barely one-sixth of an acre, with no cattle, no crop, just a few ornamental bushes.

The bushes are trimmed weekly.

The driveway is swept every two or three days.

Sarah will occasionally take to her knees with a pair of scissors to trim the edge where her front sidewalk bisects her lawn.

Not garden clippers; sewing scissors.

My wife's grandfather, Raphael Colanzi, also had a habit of dropping to his knees and prying out dandelions. Renita has fond memories of her grandpop piling her and her sisters into his car and driving country roads outside of Philadelphia, stopping at open fields to harvest the dandelion greens, a delicacy he called "chee-korry."

He scooped the weeds up with a pen knife, filling two to three paper grocery bags during the course of an afternoon. At home, Renita's mother and grandmother would sever the roots, soak the dandelion greens in the kitchen sink (using salt to detach any insects), and add them to that evening's dinner salad.

The jagged dandelion leaves resemble spinach, only are far more bitter.

The yellow flower of the dandelion is actually a cluster of more than a hundred tiny flowers called "ray florets." Eventually, these florets mature, drop away, and leave behind the parachute-like seeds that form the fluffy white puffballs. As a kid, I found dandelions to be wondrous. The yellow buds were the first flowers we would pick for our mothers, and eventually someone showed us how to split the stems and make dandelion chain necklaces.

The name dandelion may come from the Greek word *leontodon* or from the old French *dent-de-lion*, both of which translate to lion's teeth, presumably a reference to the saw-toothed leaves.

In modern French the plant is known as *pissenlit*, which means "urinate in bed," a reference to the plant's diuretic properties. "Pissabeds" is an English folk name for the plant.

Had I known of these nicknames a boy, I would have liked the dandelion even more.

Dandelions germinate asexually, without cross-fertilization. The deep root that makes them so difficult to pull cleanly from our lawns allows them to access water and nutrients other plants can't reach. They flower quickly, irregularly. Eventually the flowers transform into puffballs—those parachute-rigged seeds. When the wind comes, they easily travel hundreds of yards in search of new soil.

Someone likely brought the first dandelion to North America in the tread of a shoe or tucked in the fold of a jacket, and the weed/flower headed west with impressive speed and tenacity. The dandelion favors disrupted ground, so when a field was turned for farming, a railroad right-of-way was cleared, or a hillside was freshly logged, the dandelion appeared, and thrived, and eventually dominated.

But it is not invasive—not in the sense that it crowds out other plants or competes with native species to dominate a wild area. The dandelion moves only into human-disturbed areas. And the flowers serve as a valuable early-season nectar source for bees.

What I haven't told Sarah is that I am actually *growing* dandelions—on purpose—in more or less straight rows, just three or four inches from the fence that separates our backyards.

Renita's memories motivated me to study catalogs until I found seeds for the Italian dandelion, essentially the same as our native "weed," but slower to flower, with longer leaves.

The US Department of Agriculture estimates that a serving of uncooked dandelion greens offers up to 280 percent of our daily requirement of beta carotene and more than half the requirement of vitamin C. The dandelion root is one of the most popular herbal remedies, thought to reduce liver swelling and jaundice, and help indigestion.

Plus, the leaves taste so good in a salad, but especially sautéed in olive oil with strong garlic. Add some Italian bread, some tofu or chicken for protein, and you have a meal. ◆

Fear Cooking

KIM FOSTER

Saturday night, around midnight, I made my thirteen-year-old vegan daughter a bowl of fried rice and tofu. I made it because she was hungry.

I got out the cooked medium-grain rice, the soft tofu, the oil, then soy sauce, scallions, cabbage, carrots, cilantro, spicy chili crisp, lime, salt, and my smallest carbon-steel wok, and got to work.

I didn't have to cook for Lucy at midnight. And truly, I had every reason to say no. But these days, she is almost always mad at me. No. Not mad. Raging. She is a fiery, lava-spitting, opinionated, uncensored volcano always on the verge of erupting and frying us all.

"I can't wait to move away from this family!" she often screeches at us now, usually with a door slam, and hurls herself face-first into her bed.

Only a few hours before, she had raged at me because there was a sink full of dishes and she couldn't find a clean glass. She wasn't just lamenting the glass, she was skewering my failings as a mom. She was vicious about the state of my housekeeping. Which, when I'm writing a lot, is questionable, I admit.

She punctured me.

I know her anger isn't about me or my inability to just hit the Go button on the dishwasher (why is that so hard for me?). It's thirteen. It's hormones. It's striking off on her own. She is starting to leave me. I already can see the day, in my head, she moves out for the last time. It's years away, but close.

There isn't a lot of time for me to spend being the enemy.

So I made the rice. And I delivered it to her, steaming, in her room, in a warm bowl with a fork. Not a spoon. Not chopsticks. Not a ceramic Chinese spoon, like I like to use. Nope. A fork. She has her own way. She prefers to eat fried rice with a fork, because she has more control of her food, she told me once. So fork it is.

"I like how crunchy it is," she said, taking a bite.

I added lots of crunch because I know she has food texture issue—nothing slimy, or remotely slimelike. I added sesame seeds, chia seeds, flax seeds, toasted sticky rice, crispy fried shallots.

She smiled. I smiled. That bowl of rice gave us both a reprieve. A place to begin again.

This was a good use of my middle-of-the-night.

Lucy wants her freedom. And I will give it, doling it out a little at a time over the following months and years, until there is no more freedom to give her because she has earned it, won it, taken it. But when she asks me to make vegan tofu fried rice for her at midnight, I'm going to fucking do it.

It's fear cooking. I know. But I'm doing it anyway. ◆

That's What We Said: Public Versus Private Eating

LOUISE KRUG

*Note: **After getting a comment** about how I ate at a picnic ("You're sure eating enough, aren't you?"), I asked the question: "Do you eat the same in public as you do in private? What is hard for you about food?" on Facebook. Below are some of the responses.*

One of us didn't understand the question.

One of us said that at home, they looked up how healthy something was before she ate it. They never ate a meal alone growing up because they had such a big family, but now they ate alone all day long, and that was weird. When they ate in public, they were influenced by whom they were with, and if it was their spouse and teenage stepdaughter, they were encouraged to eat the most unhealthy thing on the menu and teased for eating "rabbit food." If they were out with their mom, however, it was just the opposite, and their mother always asked about how their weight loss was going.

Another one of us agreed with the person above, and said that when they were out to eat and sharing appetizers with friends, they had to focus and not eat more than their share of the food. They said they often wondered, and even got annoyed, when their friends weren't eating more of the delicious things in front of them.

One of us said they "treated themselves" way more in public versus private. For example, they would never sit around at home drinking jumbo margaritas and eating a gallon of queso with chips, but put them in a Mexican restaurant and it was like they had no control.

One of us said the idea of someone watching them eat in public was terrifying, and they hated eating in public.

One of us said it was just hard not to obsess.

One of us said they tried to eat neater in public unless it was tacos.

Another one said they were told by a coworker that they ate sushi wrong.

Another said they hated the commentary from others about why they didn't want to eat something—say, a piece of cake at a party. If someone said, "Oh come on, you can splurge just this once!" they made it suddenly about weight, when maybe they just didn't want cake for whatever reason. Three of us "liked" that comment.

Another one said they ate hot wings by themselves at home, and they were glad nobody was watching.

And another one of us said when they ate something like drive-through tater tots or Sour Patch Kids in their car, they destroyed the evidence.

Another one of us chimed in that on the John Tesh radio show, he talked about how research showed what someone ordered at a restaurant was affected by what their server looked like. So, for example, if your server was overweight, you would order an unhealthy dish, but not if you had a thin, healthy server. They said they found it interesting. ◆

Peanut Butter and Mustard Sandwiches

JOEL LONG

I'm sure that we ran out of jelly or jam—they were both the same to me then and pretty much now, but I had peanut butter and some version of Eddy's bread, white and spongy, squared-off slices. But we had no jelly. Honey was not yet an option I considered, so I looked in the fridge and found another sandwich condiment: not mayonnaise—that would be gross—but mustard.

I was five or six then, before kindergarten. My grandma Mary took care of me while my mom went to work for B and C Realty, by the A&W root beer stand. I'd spend the day with Grandma, helping her weed the garden, watching *Dark Shadows* on the black-and-white TV, or sometimes going to the City Bar, where I could drink a Shirley Temple while she drank a highball in the smoky dark of a bar afternoon. She was a white-haired lady by the time I knew her, with a tinge of blue from her permanents. She walked with a bit of a waddle, a bit of a paunch rounded beneath her polyester slacks. She seemed to hum but never really musically, just a hum as she did something, as she made sandwiches in the kitchen or poured milk from the carton into a tall glass. I liked the one from Ayrshire Dairy with a faded painted cow on the carton.

For lunch, Grandma made me sandwiches. I liked the deviled ham sandwiches because the ham came in one of those little cans with a red devil and his trident, and I liked the thin, salty layer of ham on the bread. When Grandma made peanut butter and jelly she'd share a sandwich with me, cutting the sandwich in triangles on the white plate and sitting with me at the Formica table next to the pantry in her kitchen. I loved it when she made liverwurst sandwiches with mayonnaise or bologna sandwiches with yellow mustard slathered against the pink meat with the skin peeled off, again on that stick-to-the-top-of-your-mouth-and-scrape-it-off-with-your-fingernail white bread. But this day, I had peanut butter, and my mind was set on it. There was the jar of French's mustard hiding behind the milk carton. I took the cold jar in my hand and set it on the counter, opened it, and swept a dollop of mustard out with a butter knife, suspending the mustard over the counter as I dropped it onto the bread. On the other piece of bread, I spread a smooth swath of Jif peanut butter and flipped it over onto the mustard piece. I didn't put it on a plate; I just grabbed it, with my fingers and thumb printed into the moist bread, nearly feeling the cool mustard.

The texture of the bread and the peanut butter mixed as I bit down. The sweetness of the peanut butter contrasted with citrus-spiced tang of the mustard. It was delicious! At so young an age, I had discovered my own sandwich. My mother mocked me for it, gently. While my oldest brother Jeff showed indifference to my culinary exploration, my other brothers, Jon and Jay, were grossed out by it, and through my childhood I felt pride in spreading that mustard and folding it over the peanut butter and grossing those boys out over and over, but enjoying the sandwich. The best way to gross someone out is to enjoy what you do to gross them out. I loved the peanut butter and mustard sandwich.

My brothers and I went to the City Bar last November to drink the first of the season's Tom and Jerrys. We went with my mother, who is as old now as Grandma Mary was then. It was still dark and smoky; no windows let in the light from outside. From time to time, the front door might open and some daylight might intrude and fresh air might seep in amid the smoke, but largely this was still my grandma's bar. We ordered a couple of Shirley Temples for my daughters; they gave me the cherries to eat.

Grandma Mary has been gone twenty-five years now. I am the one making sandwiches for the girls on mornings before school, turkey with mayo and Dijon mustard for Hannah, and peanut butter and jelly for Sarah. Certainly never mustard—boy, what a shock she'd have. I see my grandma and me sitting at her table with the triangle sandwiches on plates, and behind her in a frame is a calendar with a photo of the four of us boys, shimmering crew cuts and goofy smiles. She has made sandwiches, and now she is sitting down with me to eat, the bread in my mouth dissolving over my tongue. ◆

A Blonde, A Brunette

HANNAH PAIGE

"If chiropractic school fails, we could always open a restaurant," I said, kicking the fridge door shut behind me. The evening sun favoring California with long days streamed through the bay window.

"Oh?" My sister raised her eyebrows. "And what about college? You planning on flunking that too? Not very high hopes, having not even made it through tenth grade yet."

"Hey, if you flunk, I'll flunk. Solidarity, sister."

Sara laughed at me.

"If we had another sister with red hair, we could call it 'A Blonde, a Brunette, and a Redhead,' like the start of a bad joke, but with better food."

I piled the bags of shredded cheese on the counter next to her, along with a stick of butter, the flour container, and the jug of milk, all for easy access. "Your sous chef is ready," I said, grabbing a whisk from the jar on top of the stove.

She unrolled the butter stick, plopping it into the saucepan, then sprinkled in some flour, sealing the rubber lid on the container once more with a pop of the heel of her hand. She held out her hand, palm up. "Scalpel."

I giggled and handed her the whisk for the roux. She stirred viciously, eviscerating clumps of flour. I handed her the milk. She poured in rough tablespoons until the whisk glided through the cream sauce evenly, quietly. We added in handfuls of cheese, whisking, pausing, dipping a spoon in the pot and bringing it up to our lips to taste and to frown at one another only to add more cheese, more milk. When the sauce was pale orange, we sprinkled in salt and pepper and inevitably more salt, eventually folding in macaroni. The kitchen expanded with the stove's warmth and robust scents married to cutting boards and starched hands.

I handed her a fork as we sat down with our full bowls. "Loosen belt, enjoy."

I had a heavy hand with the white cheddar, and the dry saltiness of it stuck to my tongue. Sara, across the table, matched me bite for bite.

I looked at my older sister and smiled, mouth full of cheese, and she smiled back. Her blue eyes brightened and the sun streaming in even ribbons through the window illuminated her freckles, the ones I always envied.

"You know," I said, "Tim's a pretty good cook too." I took my eyes off her for a second, thinking of her fiancé, famous for his endless kitchen experiments, while I stirred a few noodles at the bottom of my bowl.

"Yeah," she said, and waited for me to look up. "So?"

"Can he make mac and cheese?"

One side of her thin lips drew into a tight, laughing corner, and she shook her head.

"Absolutely not."

"So, you won't start the restaurant with him?"

"Of course not. You're my sous chef, not him. Besides, Tim is blond and there's no joke that starts with two blondes and a redhead."

I stand in the grocery store, staring at the boxes of pasta. Manicotti noodles that my mother would stuff and bake for an hour until the noodles were soft and the cream sauce soaked through the logs of chicken and onions and the whole house smelled of garlic and casserole and being about six or seven. Lasagna noodles I remember slapping ricotta on, perched on the counter beside my mom, a task of the utmost importance. Spaghetti for Tim's date-night carbonara ("If you have to use cream in the sauce, you're doing it wrong").

And there are macaroni shells.

I stand there in the grocery store aisle with the dirty square and triangle tiles, little tile houses for little tile people, under my feet, and I think of violet perfume and blue eyes. I think of a restaurant never built.

Promises of gray hair and going together.

And Europe and a wedding bouquet, mine this time.

Fighting over the rocking chair when babies came.

I think of the kitchen and how we never say what we are thinking when we are young and certain the clock will keep ticking until we are done with its rusty and tired hands.

I reach up and grab a box of macaroni, and a tear escapes my hazel eye and drips onto the blue box, because there is no joke that starts with just a brunette. ◆

Kidney Stew in the Summer of Love

SKAIDRITE STELZER

Not many Americans like kidney stew. My immigrant family, however, taught me how delicious it could be. Soak the kidneys in salt, drain and chop, add potatoes, onion, bay leaves, carrots if you like. In a small Midwestern town, it was a touch of home.

The unappreciated organ meats, sometimes called offal by those who don't know their value, saved the day for me once. Although I am now vegetarian, I will always retain a soft spot for kidney stew.

During the Summer of Love, I was living in San Francisco, and suddenly many friends, both close and distant, wished to join me, leaving the constraints of our small-town upbringing behind.

My partner and I were renting a modest, two-story guest house behind the main house on the slope of Potrero Hill. The top floor was a finished apartment, with a single room below, where Spooner was living. Another mid-'60s escapee from Kalamazoo, Spooner was already busy perfecting the colorful crocheted berets that would provide a source of income for many years to come.

The first to move in with us was Kathy. Then Brian arrived. Next came the friends of Kathy and Brian. And, of course, the friends of friends followed. Everyone wanted to stay, they said, just until they found work and their own place. For a few weeks, this was fine, but then ... having to step over assorted people, most of them high on weed, was becoming a nuisance. And none of them offered to clean the cat litter, or even wash the dishes. All were, however, very willing to eat our food. I suggested they consider a nice commune or two just a short distance from the city, but found no takers.

I've never been a picky eater. However, unlike some of my friends, I never went to the extreme of the Adelle Davis raw liver diet (although she did have a tasty, healthful, mac-and-cheese recipe). Yes, I've sampled chocolate-covered ants and gathered roadside weeds. Only twice have I turned away from a new taste adventure. Once, in New York's Chinatown, an old man offered me the delicacy of a hundred-year-old egg. "So delicious," he said, so I took a substantial bite. I can't remember if I swallowed it, but somehow I politely left the shop without grimacing too severely. The second time was in Guadalajara, when I could not take a bite of the octopus, but that was a side-effect of morning sickness.

So, I went shopping with my best friend, Parsla (also a Latvian immigrant, who had her own place in the Mission District). Since the two of us were lunch outcasts from junior high days, when we sometimes brought tongue sandwiches for lunch, she was the perfect companion. We bought some fresh cow kidneys and the other ingredients (did I mention bay leaf?) and the pot started simmering. An interesting odor filled the kitchen.

By this time there were no other groceries in the house, the cupboards being denuded of even the pasta and rice. We each filled a bowl with the hearty stew and the two of us indulged. We made enough for a week or so. The first to leave was Kathy. Then, one by one, the uninvited guests from back home started gathering their backpacks and blankets and were gone. My partner tried a sip or two out of obligation, but in the end, it was just Parsla and me, sharing the leftovers with the cats.

Spooner stayed in his room below and continued crocheting. ◆

Tortilla Chips

ERIN RENEE WAHL

He's sitting on the couch watching *Star Trek* when I come home. Eating tortilla chips, which I suppose is better than if he were eating regular potato chips. Those thin, greasy things come in too many flavors to be natural. I had a theory that the ones with ridges were healthier because they're thicker. I think they just catch more oil. I'm on a diet. I wish I could eat some.

In the kitchen I rope an apron around my waist and start to dice a mean yellow onion. The broken skin fizzes with acids, making my eyes water. Snagging the kitchen towel from the rack to wipe them I remember too late that I had wiped my hands on the same towel after the first cut sprayed my hands with onion piss. My eyes drip more furiously. I could fill the bathtub in a dollhouse with my tears. Telling myself they're detoxing my eyes, I keep cutting, salty drops running down my cheeks onto my chin or down the bridge of my nose, searching for a good place to drop onto the sun-bleached hair of my forearms. I finish cutting the onion and quickly mince two cloves of garlic. I wash and dry my hands, using a fresh towel to do so. I grab a tissue to blow my nose and wipe my face … not in that order. Before I start to seed the green pepper I peek around the corner of the kitchen into the living room—*Star Trek* and chips.

I want to tell him to stop eating those tortilla chips. I want to say it's just mean that he can eat a bag of tortilla chips once a week and not gain any weight. I want to say that he's hurting my feelings by eating all these tortilla chips and then abstaining from the meals I make. I want to remind him how unhealthy those chips are; maybe throw out some well-researched facts about the dangers of shoveling in too many chips. I want to scold him for leaving salsa-stained bowls around the house like dirty dropped socks. I want him to pick up those socks too. I want him to offer to cut the dreaded onion. I cannot say any of those things, because all of those things are nagging and every girlfriend knows you shouldn't nag.

Instead I try: "You should really stop eating those. I'm making dinner and you won't be able to eat any by the time I'm done. Dinner will be healthier and tastier than those anyway." A good, logical, nonchalant reason. I congratulate myself but he's heard it before, recognizes it for the nagging it is, and rolls his eyes anyway, grabbing another handful of salty chips. Captain Kirk is going to send an ensign down to the new planet with Spock and Doctor McCoy.

To be fair, the tortilla chips here are good. Most of the time I'm so busy with graduate school work that I have to settle for purchasing Santitas or Mission chips at the Fry's grocery not too far from our house. But sometimes I'll make a journey to the south part of Tucson, to a Hispanic grocery store where those in-the-know go to buy special foodstuffs. This includes several brands of locally made tortilla chips, which are probably the most delicious in the long and tasty history of corn triangles.

Annoyed, I Google tortilla chips from the swelter of the kitchen. According to Wikipedia, tortilla chips first came on the scene in the 1940s, as a way to make use of busted corn tortillas. Supposedly, Rebecca Webb Carranza was the first person to think of this particular use for the rejected tortillas, and her modest success turned into a major one and a booming business. For a long time the El Zarape Tortilla Factory got the ingredients for its tortillas and chips from a business in the south of Tucson. The location, which is now a restaurant, still retains the original silo from that business.

I've discovered a link between my little life and the tortilla chips rustling in the bag in the living room. I hear the unmistakable alarm of a phaser and the crackle of plastic announcing the closure of the chip bag. The vegetables in the wok hiss as I add tortilla chips—the good ones—to the shopping list on the fridge. ◆

Enough Is Enough

STEVEN GOFF

Enough is enough! I'm sick of catching flak for serving offal. People are always sticking their noses up at variety meats: liver, kidneys, sweetbreads, and the like. People have even called me and my restaurant "pretentious" for what we serve. But I don't want to serve everyday food.

I don't really know when cooking sustainably and using all of the animal became "pretentious," but if that's what it is, then I'm one pretentious son of a bitch. I want people who come to my restaurant to try new things, to leave having experienced something extraordinary. When a patron looks at my menu and makes a fake vomiting sound, I just want to shake the bejesus out of them. It's worse when we are serving a dish such as duck liver paté at an event and people scoff.

I know you have eaten McDonald's, or hot dogs, or other various and questionably processed foods, but you won't give a different part of a locally and sustainably raised animal a chance? To shun the noble organ meats after eating pink slime in your cheeseburger, or the assholes and elbows they process into commercially produced hot dogs ... you're not just an ignorant first-world snob, but I would guess slightly daft as well. An animal gave its life for us to eat it, so we owe it to that animal to use up every bit of it—and not just utilize each part, but also to make it a damn good meal.

The United States is the only country in the world that condones such wasteful eating habits. We're not just smacking the animal we killed in the face by not using everything, we're insulting starving people across the world. We are ignoring thousands of years and hundreds of different cultures' histories and traditions, just so we know we're eating something that we ignorantly consider "safe" or "normal." The world absolutely cannot go on the way it has for the last seventy or so years. Populations are growing exponentially, and we have to utilize everything. We cannot condone factory farming anymore. It isn't working. We can't survive or keep the planet healthy eating just poultry breast and popular cuts of steak, while discarding the rest.

We have to think about what we're eating in an intelligent fashion. Keep an open mind. When you finally let go of your false pretenses and preconceived notions about a product and give it a try, you may find it to be the best meal of your life. At least there could be a couple new go-tos in the dishes you once snubbed!

Let me put it this way: If you were killed for your meat, and I just ate your loin, then threw the rest in the trash, wouldn't you be at least a bit annoyed? You're dead and gone because I was hungry, and I didn't even bother to use everything you were made of, because I'm "above" eating things like that. Just saying. ◆

How to Make Mamaw's Biscuits

REBECCA POTTER

This weekend we were in my mother's kitchen. My mom, my sister, my grandmother, and me.

"She got tarred of me pesterin' her, so she finely let me hep her," Mamaw said. She was talking about her own mother, from a time when Mamaw was only ten or eleven. "Then she'd roll me outta bed ev'ry mornin' from then on to make biscuits." She laughed at this. Gina, my sister, gathered everything she needed to make Mamaw's biscuits: flour, oil, and buttermilk. Mamaw stood opposite my sister, on the other side of the counter, ready to give instruction.

Gina had been planning this for days. My family is going through a difficult time right now. My Papaw just spent a week in the hospital for surgery. Now he and Mamaw are staying with my parents as Papaw continues to recover. Mamaw has dementia and Alzheimer's, which complicates everything. That Gina wanted to do something to help did not surprise me. She is a nurse and has a nurse's personality: she is a caregiver and has a servant's heart. For the months before my other grandmother passed away, Gina helped care for her in countless ways. When medical emergencies arise, I usually call Gina first.

So she had decided that Mamaw would teach her how to make her homemade biscuits today. Mamaw's biscuits are famous in our family, and rightfully so. They are delicious. Golden and crispy on the bottom, fluffy and light on the top. They are perfect for jelly or gravy or just butter. They taste like my childhood, and my mother's childhood, and her mother's, and hers before her. Mamaw's biscuits taste like family and love and legacy.

That's why the recipe cannot be written down. That, and Mamaw doesn't really use a recipe. "OK, now just dump three or four cups a flour in there, or whatever, just till it looks right, ya know." But it takes a skilled and knowing eye to know what it's supposed to look like. Even the temperature of the oven is not exact. When Gina asked her what to set the oven to, Mamaw responded with, "You gotta cook 'em fast. The faster the better."

"Four fifty?" Gina asked.

"Oh, I dunno. Whatever you think. Just gotta cook 'em fast."

It requires a skilled hand to know how much the dough should be kneaded. Gina slapped the lump of dough onto the counter and pressed the heel of her hand into it, and again. Mamaw watched from the other side of the bar. "Yeah, that's right." She nodded. "Don't mess with the dough too much. But be rough. Tell that dough who's boss." As Gina slammed the dough onto the counter, Mamaw laughed, more than I had seen her laugh in weeks, maybe months, possibly years. The more instruction she gave, the more of my grandmother I saw, before her dementia made thinking and remembering difficult. She was not confused, she was not absent in her own lost thought. She was there in the kitchen with us, being useful and having fun. Gina had given her something back she hadn't felt in a long time: a purpose.

My sister continued following her instructions exactly, turning the dough just so between her hands while Mamaw looked on, her chin resting in one hand, her other hand pointing to where Gina had missed a spot. "Mmmhhm. That's right. You got it." She supervised with great importance and even greater delight. I admired the way my sister was taking care of my grandmother, how she was making her feel good, strong, and healthy. And all she needed was flour, oil, and buttermilk to do it.

Gina put the biscuits in the oven and fifteen fast minutes later, they were done. Mamaw bit into one, the crumbs falling from her lips. She closed her eyes, savoring the taste, and smiled.

"Not bad for your first time." ◆

Food Fight

JOAN SADDLER

Nine a.m.

I plop a fifteen-pound bag of mortgage files on my desk along with my equally weighted purse. "Good morning, Joan!" sing out multiple voices. The party is already at full tilt.

Residential lending employees frequently indulged in what I secretly but fondly coined "fat lady parties." Stressful jobs beg to be interrupted by distractions. Food is the perfect siren. Any excuse will do: holidays, birthdays, Tuesdays. Platters of potluck come from all corners of the workplace floor: cold-cut trays, lasagna, weird "Asian" salad with canned mandarin orange slices and crunchy La Choy noodles. Some ladies plug in Crock Pots early morning and by lunchtime serve up steaming sausage and peppers or three-layer chili.

"Can you eat this, Joan?" the concerned chili lady asks. "There's no meat!" She proudly presents a sagging paper plate of brown lumps and orange cheese. I gently declare lactose intolerance. Soda gushes like a geyser. Desserts dominate the landscape: mountains of cookies, fields of brownies, waterfalls of doughnuts. A flurry of recipes exchange excited hands: Combine one box of lemon-flavored pudding mix with one container of Cool Whip …

For the past sixteen years I've dined mostly on a balancing act of organic whole grains, beans, vegetables, fermented foods, wild-caught fish, and organic eggs, otherwise known as a macrobiotic diet.

To be sociable I tasted anything my body could handle. I still brought my regular lunch on party days.

"Don't you miss normal food?"

Denise, who prides herself on eating nothing green, gets a particular charge out of investigating my lunch and making unfiltered comments. "That looks godawful," she twangs in her flat, Midwestern accent. "Does it taste as bad as it looks?" We both crack up. Lenore declares me a fanatic who will probably die getting hit by a bus and all my nasty food will have been for naught.

The ladies enjoyed a few of my recipes. A garlicky black olive pesto with whole grain crackers was their favorite, but they found my three-bean salad shocking. "This doesn't taste like regular three-bean salad," bubbles Sara, "but I like it! Where did you buy the dressing?" I describe my recipe of toasted sesame seed oil, brown rice vinegar, brown rice syrup and fresh dill. Her eyes glaze over. "Well, very good!" she cheerfully murmurs mid-chew and waddles away. Most like nibbling at whatever I bring. "I feel so healthy!" they giggle.

One day Kara shyly approaches my desk. "Any advice for constipation?" she whispers. Explaining how to cook adzuki beans is out of the question. "Do you eat any greens?" I ask.

"You mean like salad? I eat a huge salad every day!" she cries, clearly exasperated that this effort is not working. I imagine her probable salad of pale iceberg lettuce, anemic hothouse tomatoes, and colon-clogging ranch dressing.

"How about broccoli?" I ask. Kara leaves with a prescription: Steam two cups of fresh broccoli for five minutes, drizzle with olive oil and soy sauce, and eat daily.

A day or so later she returns. "Broccoli is my new friend," she beams.

Others begin coming to me with questions and comments. "How did you manage to not catch that nasty bug we all got?" Mostly my advice goes unheeded. "You're so lucky to be thin!" I find that laughable and annoying. "If you ate what I ate, you would be thin, too!" I retort. "No, you're just lucky. It's your metabolism," they admonish, reaching for peanut M&M's on a neighboring desk.

At an annual eye checkup, I have to update my medical history. "You're not on *any* medications?" questions the technician. Affirmative. She looks again at the birthdate, confirming I'm indeed at the age where I should be medicated for *something*. "Wow, you're really lucky."

Recently I attended a reunion with some of the ladies. "Oh my god, you haven't changed a bit!" they cry. Denise now has emphysema and diverticulitis. Another lady is diabetic. Almost all have gained significant weight and take what they sheepishly label "happy pills."

"Guess you were right about that crazy diet," they marvel. Excited to hear this admission, I launch into details about the cooking classes I now teach. "Many conditions can be helped and even reversed with the right foods!" I encourage. They indulge me with a wan smile.

Some might attend. If they're lucky. ◆

Early Thanksgiving

CYNTHIA BELMONT

The steak we are eating is dusky rare, scantily peppered, stripped from the deer hanging in our garage, from alongside her spine. I shot her this afternoon and now she hangs by her neck where the car usually sits, dripping from her enormous cavity. It was cold enough at last light that I was forced to leave the field to warm my fingers in the truck vent before I could cut her open, steaming in the dark woods. It was a difficult kill. I had to finish it in her neck at ten yards as she watched me calmly, paralyzed by my first shot, and when the bullet hit her windpipe she exhaled a loud, gray puff of breath that I will never forget; it hangs in the air still, it will always hang in the air under that shaggy spruce, it is her ghost.

She was a colossus—a mature northern white-tailed doe, perhaps 180 pounds, mother of how many springs of fawns, denizen of pine, birch, and cedar woodland on the south shore of Lake Superior. Her hooves left deep dewclaw prints in the snow. Her eyes froze quickly; the frozen night-vision pupils of deer are radiant icicles shaped like star sapphires in black domes of sky.

The interior back muscle of deer is called the fish loin. In cows we call it filet mignon, but this is not cow, this is nothing like cow, I got this meat after sitting for hours in a silent winter landscape whose only distraction was evolving painterly clouds. My friend crouched, holding her back legs, as I field-dressed her by headlamp, wrestling with her thick uterus and great pillows of organ fat. I dragged her flopping, heavy corpse 200 yards to the road along a rough track at the forest verge by myself because, girl hunter, I insist. Venison tastes better than beef anyway, regardless of all this labor, because it is rich and complex, musky purple muscle that leapt streams.

It's the opening Saturday of hunting season, Thanksgiving week, and what we are eating is gratitude, praise, since deer live in no other way. Grazing, dashing, listening—dear life is evident in every poised, decorous movement of their bodies, which are amply meaningful because each white-tail is an individual with a personal history known to the others, and to the woods where they trampled, marked, gnawed. Deer are made of acorns, shoots, twigs, sweet leaves, and so are we, then, also made of the woods.

In the coming days our kitchen will be about one thing, and that is taking care of her carcass—sectioning quarters, severing roasts and steaks from the silverskin that would make them gamy, sorting scraps for sausage and dog food, packaging with clean white paper and tape. My lover does all this herself; my lover is patient, and her hands are strong and red and precise with the boning knife. Blood everywhere, smeared on the counter, clotting in buckets, mixing with hers in the cuts on her hands. She will cook all this meat over the course of the year, starting with tonight's steak, each preparation a reminder of this day.

The sharp, spicy, singular smell of deer blood evokes iced hay crackling under my boots. It evokes the camouflaged form of my friend subtly shifting fifty yards to the north, crows gathering on a blowdown in the flat bright of midday, pink tongue drooping from a dainty muzzle, bourguignonne that my lover makes that is the finest food on Earth.

Mainly the smell calls up the chemicals that streak through the hunter when a deer is suddenly standing in a gap between trees, in a space that did not register as space before it was filled by this unbelievable, actual presence. It calls up the imperative to move, to shoot—the fluttery crushing charge of the terrible instant. The thrill and the sorrow one swallows after killing.

This season's blood is a story of a grand dame. Queen of the woods. Like every doe who walks free on venerable trails, licks the salt from the new day, and feeds us where we are. ◆

Dinner for One

MARK LEWANDOWSKI

Spinning away from the slopes of the Acropolis, the narrow, winding streets of the Plaka feature a plethora of little shops and restaurants. It's a great place to wind down after a full day of sightseeing. One night for dinner, I sat down to a garden salad and a heap of *frutti di mare* nestled on a bed of freshly made linguini tinged yellow with saffron. The restaurant was open to the street. As I savored my pasta, I watched the passersby. One happened to be a dog. There are thousands of strays in Athens. This fella seemed to be one. He stopped about ten feet from my table, across the way from the closet-sized jewelry store sharing a wall with the restaurant. He kept his gaze on the jewelry store as people strolled past him. After five minutes or so a woman came out of the jewelry store with a large plate of food. It wasn't dog food, I think. Could have been a healthy pile of lamb. She set the plate in front of the dog, patted his head, and went back to the store.

The dog dug in, but slowly, apparently not concerned about other strays happening along. As he ate, a homeless man approached. I'd seen him before, rooting through a garbage can near the Acropolis Museum. He had long hair and a scraggly beard, a pair of torn and stained cords, and a winter coat and boots held together with packing tape. He gripped a plastic shopping bag, likely containing whatever he found in the garbage; it didn't look that full. I feared he'd stop at the restaurant and ask for a handout. Or just stare. What would I do? Offer him some bread?

The homeless man never even looked in my direction. Instead, as he walked by the jewelry store, he looked down at the dog's dinner and licked his lips, then continued down the sloping cobblestones, his gaze fixed on the path life had laid out for him.

Soon after, the woman from the jewelry store picked up the now clean plate and the dog waddled away. My waiter cleared my table, and a few minutes later he came back with my gelato: a scoop each of hazelnut, chocolate and vanilla. I spun the cold metal bowl to the vanilla and considered the weight of this most simple of pleasures. ◆

Bananas

CECILIA GIGLIOTTI

The summer after sophomore year you bake a lot of banana bread. Loaves upon loaves upon loaves. You could have been Jesus's supplier. Camped out in the kitchen, slicing and dicing, half driven to tears by the pungence of naturally occurring sugar. So strong that you use a fraction of the brown sugar listed in the recipe. Too sweet otherwise. Like the month you spent with the boy at the beginning of spring semester, a confectionery of words and embraces, movies and songs. Five months ago but still pungent enough to reach you. That stuff will rot your teeth if you're not careful. According to your mom. At first you don't bake without her, and then, before you know it, you're mixing and pouring and shaping batter at all hours, enveloped in yourself, a packet of shortening. You'll gain weight this summer, because of all this, but that's probably for the best; the doctor would have said you were on the verge of taking up too little space as you were, if you'd seen the doctor. Anyways, you're sick of disappearing. It's time to make it harder for someone like him to hold you, to mold you, to fold you like so much dough. It's time to take up more space. The bananas are certainly taking up space in the house—invading it, infesting it. They come so cheap this time of year. Why not take what you can get? No yeast required, either: once baked through, the flour is dense, closing in around medallions of banana, gooey and gummy. The complete mass is dark, browned like your sister who spends her days in the sunshine, who has not been hurt, who is not afraid. Sometimes you toss in a handful of walnuts for a bit of crunch, a bit of resistance. No one in your house is allergic, and even if you were it would be worth it. Five months ago was cotton candy, unsubstantial, empty. This will satisfy you. ◆

Valentine

ALISON TOWNSEND

It's the middle of winter, but tonight I am in summer's warm arms, Boston lettuce torn in half before me for a salad. You're at the stove, stirring Indonesian sweet potato peanut soup. I'm at the sink, staring down into pale green whorls. "The heart's the best part," my mother says, a thousand Junes ago. Then a breath and I'm back, the moment sliding past, a window raised inside me, the hearts of the world lined up like schoolchildren waiting for the bus.

Hearts of palm, artichoke hearts, the heart of the country, hearts of darkness, heart songs, heartthrobs, pour your heart out, wear your heart on your sleeve, set your heart free like the old Judy Collins song said, lose heart, take heart, the Havahart traps we used to catch rats, the death of the heart, the heart is a lonely hunter, Joan of Arc's heart that was too pure to burn, the deer hoof prints pressed like hearts in snow, the heart-shaped rock my friend found on top of a mountain one month after her husband died.

In fifth grade I wrote a fifty-page, handwritten report called "A Short History of the Human Heart," as if, with my colored pencils and tracing paper, I knew everything there was to say on the subject. And aren't we all experts? Aren't we all beginners when it comes to the heart, its four chambers never big enough to contain us, though we haven't room for more? It takes so much work to get to the heart of the matter, a red fruit at the core of each conversation, little bonfires leaping between us when we kiss or hug or even just shake hands.

When I was little I had to recite poems by heart at school, memorizing them with my body while the fist in my chest punched at my ribs. It's still the same today, my heart in my throat whenever I speak; the feeling is always red. I know my husband's face by heart too, and that of the daughter I never had, though I have nearly forgotten my mother's, dead when I was a child. My engagement ring has two gold hands holding a gold heart, as did my mother's, though my husband did not know that when he chose it. I wear the tip pointed toward my own heart, according to tradition; it is a sign I am taken.

My father once helped me make a clay heart for a science fair project. Larger than life-size, it hung on a metal stand, wired with lights that mimicked a pulse. I didn't win a prize, not even honorable mention. I don't know what happened to the heart I'd spent a whole weekend molding and painting. When my father died, there was no autopsy, so we never knew for certain if it was his head or his heart. But when I stood in the room where he'd fallen, when I lay my body down over the place where they'd found him, to touch what he'd touched last, I knew. It was his heart, the only muscle we say can be "broken."

In the '60s, there was a salad called "hearts of lettuce," iceberg wedges topped with Thousand Island dressing. No one eats it now. No one even buys iceberg lettuce. I still don't know why the heart is the best part, though my mother never lied about anything. Or why we say *lub-dub, lub-dub* to describe the sound the heart makes, the small ocean of the body ebbing and flowing, rocking us each on the water, the way it did when I memorized poems: as if to say *I rise, I fall, I rise again. I rise, I fall, I'm gone.* ◆

Edible Gifts

CHRISTINE PERKINS-HAZUKA

I flew from Connecticut to California in June to attend Auntie Maggie's ninety-fifth birthday celebration. Her birthdate was May 21, but the party was postponed so more people could make it—"more people" meaning me, I'm pretty sure.

Maggie was my godmother, my father's second elder sister, and the most immaculate housekeeper I knew, which says a lot because our family made a competition of neatness. One Thanksgiving turned into a refrigerator/oven cleaning frenzy when Auntie Maggie and Auntie Madeline discovered that my aging grandmother had lost her edge in the fastidious department. Drinking was involved to be sure, and Gomi, the only sober adult present, sat like an angry Sphinx glaring daggers at her disrespectful daughters. She sulked for years.

Auntie Maggie was also a good cook. I remember being in her house for dinner once, watching as she stood at the white Formica counter, red pedal pushers fitting snugly to her trim figure, red-and-white striped shirt tucked in, a crisp white apron tied around her tiny waist. Deftly she placed floured, egg-coated, bread-crumb-dipped chicken legs, thighs, and breasts into Wesson oil, brought to just the right temperature in her spotless electric skillet. The chicken sizzled and popped, but the paper towel-covered counter and the newspaper-strewn floor remained oil free. The chicken appeared on the table golden brown, expertly displayed in the folds of paper towels—an edible gift. Sitting at the sparkling chrome and grey table, I watched her serve whipped, not mashed, potatoes, with pools of butter, not margarine, melting in the mounds. There was also green salad with tomato wedges, rings of red onions, and cubed bell peppers (none of which I liked, but they looked pretty), and real Wish-Bone Italian dressing in a glass bottle with all offending fingerprints wiped away. And there was apple pie on the counter—the kind of homemade pie with so many apple slices that the crust made little rolling hills, sparkling with sugar crystals in the fluorescent light.

How unfair life was. My cousins Kathy and Eddie ate something comparable to this every night. At my house fried chicken was an oily mess of blackened skin and greasy flesh presented on an equally greasy mound of paper towels. Sometimes we had a greyish meat loaf without onions (my father detested them), or oregano, or basil, not even lowly parsley, but with a thick stripe of red-orange catsup across the top, and a salad of iceberg lettuce and garbanzo beans. My mother's thrifty "Thousand Island" dressing was catsup stirred into mayo. Never, ever was there homemade dessert, and only rarely Neapolitan ice cream (how I loved those nights).

Our house was almost as clean as Auntie Maggie's, though much smaller, older, and on the "poor" side of town. My mother had married at seventeen and had me that same year; Maggie married at twenty-five and didn't have children for three years. My dad drove a 7Up truck; Auntie Maggie's husband was a dental technician. Mother almost always had a job outside the home; Maggie never did. Mommy sort of tried to be a good cook, and when she failed, my father teased until she cried. Tears were her only weapon against criticism, and they worked marginally well. They stayed married until she died at seventy-eight.

Like much else about Auntie Maggie's life, her ninety-fifth party seemed idyllic to me. Cousin Kathy had turned into an only slightly less meticulous cook than her mom. My godmother, who could be an unfair critic, as perfectionists are, was uncharacteristically humble and grateful at her birthday dinner, and cried publicly for only the second time I can remember (my father made her cry the first time). "Thank you, thank you," she mumbled over and over to the more than thirty party guests.

In the old days, when everything was spotless and her fried chicken better than anyone's, Maggie was as harsh a critic as my father, and even more cynical and cruel. "Uncle Joey is such a pig. He never cleans his filthy bathroom ... Kathy is going to get fat like Uncle Joey's sister Alice ... Eddie will wet the bed until he's in high school ... I'd have more kids if they'd look like me, not dark Mexicans like Joey." She harped on these themes endlessly.

Yes, there was a price to pay for that fried chicken and homemade pie.

I would have gladly paid it. ◆

Holy Bread

THAD DEVASSIE

I.

I sold a slice of Holy Bread on eBay for a buck fifty. To be fair, it was a slice of focaccia, the top bread layer of my chicken curry sandwich, roughly the thickness of Texas toast and cut into a perfect triangle, its innards painted the mustard tint of liquefied curry powder. This alone does not make it Holy Bread, but rather it was the bite I lopped off the left side of the risen isosceles that, with the precision of my teeth and angular chisel of my upper lip, carved out the likeness of a holiday conifer. There they were, pecan shavings embedded into the bread representing gifts of the Magi, a small manger near the base of the tree. It's quite something to see the promise of eternal life in the underbelly of a sandwich slice during lunch hour. To be fair, this is not good evangelism.

II.

The prize was perfectly sealed on a white ceramic plate with translucent pink Saran Wrap. It was tastefully photographed with an artful description. I had to use a friend's account, for I had no dealings in Internet commerce. This guy Gene who I work with bought it as a favor, a joke, perhaps a gift, but certainly an insult considering his nominal bid. He could've saved me a great deal of trouble with all that Internet stuff. I haven't visited the Holy Bread, but Gene's wife tells me it rests near the head of their formal table, the one nobody sits at for meals, atop an antique sideboard, free of mold, pure as the day it was conceived.

III.

Recently, two sisters from Virginia posted a corn flake for sale on eBay resembling a perfect likeness of the state of Illinois. No miracle, no leap of faith, just dumb luck straight out of the box. The flake fetched $1,350. I've never been a fan of the land of Lincoln and now I'm led to believe that Virginia is for scammers. I'll be spending Christmas this year with Gene and his family. I'll be the one sitting at the head of the table with a well-sealed slice of divine intervention. ◆

Feeding Time

CRIS MAZZA

The table was set with all seven dishes stacked at the head where my father sat. Everyday stoneware for weekdays, china on Sundays. Hot pads, to protect the plastic tablecloth that protected the vinyl table covers that protected the wood surface, likewise were only in front of his place. When the serving dishes (very seldom a pot straight from the stove) were put on the table, we were all already seated, three on one side, two on the other, and Mom at the other end. Dad dished the food onto each plate, starting with the youngest. For any solid meat other than pork chops or chicken, he would have to carve it first, right there at the table, then he put portions onto each plate, one at a time. Even steak was sliced and doled out, followed by the vegetable (often exotic ones like eggplant, artichoke, or squash flowers), and potato or rice. He passed each plate to the nearest of us, who passed it along to its intended. Usually he would say the name of whosoever's plate it was when he first passed it, even though it seemed to always go youngest to oldest, so he could keep track of portions. It's not supposed to sound like a scene from Charles Dickens. We were allowed to talk, even ask for another serving. We also had our manners corrected, sometimes our opinions too. After the main course came salad, which he tossed—adding the oil and vinegar—and served the same way he had the meal. With both the main meal and the salad, but more the salad because it was always tossed, he had to be aware of which parts some of us would not eat, and decide if the battle was worth waging. He'd long stopped trying to get me to eat liver or fresh tomato. Dessert (usually ice cream) might be served in the kitchen and brought in by our mother. But a few times a year, we had a whole fresh coconut for dessert. My father asked the closest one of us to hold the coconut steady while he used a hand-cranked wood drill to bore two holes through the shell, in the natural indentations that seemed made for this purpose. He poured the milk directly from the coconut into seven little dishes. Mysterious how he knew how much milk the coconut would hold, but it never ran dry before the seventh dish received its portion.

Then, holding the coconut in one hand, he wielded a hammer to break the shell like an egg. From the two halves, he used a long knife to pry out jagged irregular selections of white meat lined on one side with the brown casing of the shell. He put these pieces into the dishes with the milk and passed them around. Silverware had all been cleared from the table after the salad. We crunched the coconut and sipped the milk directly from the dishes. Then Dad pried additional pieces from the shell and offered them to whoever wanted more, reaching down the table with glistening white coconut meat speared on the end of his knife. We plucked chunks off the blade with our fingers ◆.

Maynard, Now Gone

CATHY ROSE

When I think of Uncle Maynard, I think of ham, salty Smithfield ham, pig shanks half the size of me, one laid out on the dinner table, the other wrapped in cotton and tied with twine for us to take home. When my father's father died, he left seven children to fend for themselves, and it was Maynard, the eldest, who'd taken their father's failing hog business, there in the three-store town of Walters, Virginia, and turned it into a thriving industry. It was Maynard's business that put my father through the university, that bought my Uncle Frank a general store after he lost his arm from hanging it too far out the window of his pickup one drunken night, and it was Maynard's business that supported my Aunt Lucille when her leg swelling got so bad she couldn't keep her job at the mill.

"Can you carry the ham to the boot, little lady?" Maynard said to me when I was still a very little girl. He called the trunk the boot. All the country relatives did. I remember the sheer weight of the beast in my arms, the thud as I dropped it in our trunk, and the excitement at Maynard's attention toward me. He was a striking man, taller than my father—with jet-black hair, thick and wavy and parted just shy of center, and his teeth, which fascinated me, were short and perfectly straight across, like someone had taken a saw to them. Maynard was a farmer, with a garden out back, but he dressed like a Southern gentleman, in crisp, white, short-sleeve shirts and dress slacks up high around his waist, not under his paunch as the others did. Sometimes Maynard wore suspenders, but the thin ones you see under the suit coats of businessmen.

"They drive into Norfolk to shop for clothes," my mother said approvingly of Maynard and his wife. She hated my father's ties to his relatives on the other side of the James, just a ferry ride from our town, but culturally worlds away. Over the years, she warmed toward Maynard, and even grew to admire him. It wasn't lost on her that Maynard, while he'd only moved one house down from where he and my father and all the others had been raised, even though he'd married an uneducated girl (by necessity, they say), in many ways was the cosmopolitan man my own father had never quite become.

But there was one year it was hard visiting Maynard. It was after a hippie teacher from my high school introduced me to tofu and yoga and her Sikh guru from up in D.C. I'd become a yogi with a mantra and had been a strict vegetarian for months when our family made the drive to the country, and on the way there, it wasn't only me who was concerned what my ham uncle would think. "Why do you always have to be so different?" my father said as we pulled onto the ferry. He was having a harder and harder time with me, and now this new vegetarian embarrassment. "It'll be fine," my mother said, annoyed with my father but at the same time not certain herself what would happen. Even my brother, normally indifferent to my problems, seemed nervous for me.

The table was set when we arrived, and my aunt had us eat right away, before the food got cold. A TV dinner family, we looked forward to these meals, and laid out were all our favorite dishes: the spoonbread, the collards, my aunt's special tomato pudding. But our eyes were fixed on the centerpiece, Maynard's perfect shank of Smithfield ham, thinly sliced at one end so as to be all ready for our plates.

"I do not want this ham," I told myself, and in that moment, I really don't think I did. I was a proud ascetic, steadfast in my convictions, but more than that, I was too worried what Maynard thought of me now. I knew my father had told him.

But then I saw the man my mother had come to know. Our Atticus Finch—he gathered us around the table, and after he'd said his traditional grace, Maynard, with that reach, that easy manner, just turned to my father.

"Roy, pass this lovely young lady the butter beans, fresh picked from our garden this morning. I reckon she'll enjoy those." ◆

Go Ahead, Break Me

AMY NAWROCKI

Growing up, I never liked eggs, especially the yolks. I blame this on over-poaching and hard boiling. Also Easter. In my mind are movies of my siblings and me watching a wafer of blue or pink dye dissolve into a cup of water. Next, we turned the ten-minute eggs to coat them evenly. The gaudy neon artifacts found their way into centerpieces and baskets of frizzy green plastic grass. Mom even baked colored eggs into Easter babka. If there were egg hunts, I've forgotten them, and all that remain are visions of dye-soaked yolks, grey-green and chalky. For many years, into my adult life, these unappetizing eggs turned me off yolks, unless the hateful center was whipped unrecognizably into a watery scramble.

Maybe it was a diner special of eggs Benedict; maybe a traditional English breakfast with fried egg, grilled tomato, beans, and black pudding. Maybe it was the Korean food truck cook who managed a half-dozen fried eggs on a flat grill and placed each on the top of *bibimbap*, one of which was mine. When a perfect sun breaks over a field of color, you just go with it.

When I first began to cook on my own, I surrendered to the convenience of nonstick pans and silicone poaching pods. Porcelain egg cups gave me perfect, soft-boiled treats, sprinkled with salt and pepper, julienned basil. Before long, I was a convert: poached egg on miso toast; over-easy laid gently onto sautéed brussels sprouts; bacon's sunny friend. Separated, whisked, then reunited into the fluffiest omelet.

Even as I became more adventurous as a cook and eater, I still held onto lackadaisical resignation. I'm no expert, after all, double tapping the shell against the teakettle's handle, opening the edges with two hands. For poaching, I resisted giving up the gadgets. Disasters happened—overdone centers or a cup swamped by an excited boil. I cursed imprecise electric coils and stubborn mechanical timers. As it turned out, I had it all wrong, checking like an expectant mother under stainless steel lids, picking out broken shells and claiming victory in status quo, in good enough. Maybe this is when expertise really begins, when the novice acknowledges she's afraid.

One day, when I'm feeling bold, I give in to the watched pot and wait for transference. I stand over the stove and try to count the barely open bubbles that begin to congregate like unhatched tadpoles at the bottom of the pan. They bounce open at the edge of liquid, losing the air that held them solid. As if I'm the one to do it, as if I've asked nicely enough not to be refused, the water comes to a boil, a smooth simmer. I drop in a teaspoon of vinegar because this time I really mean it. Then, as instructed, I create a whirlpool, spinning my carefully selected slotted spoon like Poseidon in an untied apron. It's almost too much for me to set the timer. It's almost too much to crack the egg, to trust. I hold my breath. The broken egg spills into the water and doesn't disperse or stretch out talons of white disorganization. Instead, it holds itself together in opaque serenity. At the three-minute bell, I rescue it from the water bath, place the cloud on waiting toast, and prick the saffron center with the tines of my fork.

Masters of any discipline will talk of revelation and epiphany, the moment when everything changes. On this day, let's say it's Sunday, one perfect egg. Go ahead, break me. Send me to spin in unsalted pools. Sop me up with your peasant bread; you know you want to. Trust the whirlpool ◆

Eating America

RICHARD LeBLOND

My comfort food is meat loaf and mashed potatoes at truck stop cafes. I am an old roadie (seventy-eight and counting, with luck), and every summer I head west from my home in North Carolina. Roadside eateries are more than just food stops. They are the holdouts of the beefy, high-carb meals fed to me by Mom at supper, and Grandma on Sunday afternoons.

One recent summer, at the outset of a western voyage, I decided to eat regional foods wherever I was at day's end. I should have abandoned the project after the first day, as it was a lesson in American obesity. That evening, in Indiana, I asked the motel clerk if he could recommend a restaurant that served regional food. Maybe something from the German heritage.

He sent me to a "boiled chicken dinner" in Oldenburg, where all the streets are "Strasse." I envisioned chicken parts swimming in a broth, but instead I was served half a chicken that had been boiled—not in water, but in a deep pool of oil—with its one side dish, a bushel of french fries. From my seat at the counter, I could see the vittles roiling in an iron skillet the size of a small swimming pool.

Next evening, in Amana, Iowa, I was sent to a restaurant run by the Ebenezer Society, a Germanic communal colony that settled there in 1856. Dinner was served family-style at large tables, where I was seated with perfect (and maybe a few imperfect) strangers. A steady stream of transporters brought plates and bowls filled with meats, breads, mashed and boiled potatoes, and side dishes of every vegetable grown in Iowa—what my grandparents called trimmings. Eventually, there were two large plates and seven bowls in front of me. And that was before dessert. In two days, I had eaten my weight.

Seated next to me was a Mrs. Weekley, fifteen years widowed. She told me she still had "his and her" tractors (I wondered whether this was a Midwestern pickup line), and that she gets on the John Deere mower "whenever the urge arises" (and I stopped wondering).

Now that my stomach had been noticeably expanded, I figured I was ready for the "Mountain G'oat" breakfast in East Glacier, Montana, in spite of the awful pun. I was served a loaf of oats about the shape, size, and weight of a brick, baked with apricots, raisins, and egg ("for strength," said the waitress), and topped with a local huckleberry sauce. I think it is still lodged in my body.

Big helpings are the norm at roadside diners, and sometimes big helpings are taken to an extreme, offering a meal so large that if the eater can eat it all, it's free. I found such a meal in the middle of nowhere, Silver Lake, Oregon. The cafe served mostly ordinary fare—burgers and fries—but there were a few oddities, like alligator nuggets and fries, and a four-ounce gator burger for kids. I was told the gators were shipped from Louisiana "overnight," though the nearest airport was almost a hundred miles away.

On the wall behind the counter were six photographs of large young men. They were the six men who apparently believed their bodies were amusement parks, and tried to eat the "Double Big Hoss!!!" It was a sandwich so large I think all of them must now be dead from ruptured plumbing.

Only one, a logger, succeeded in eating all of this vertical buffet. Between the halves of a six-inch bun were "2½ lbs. beef, ½ lb. bacon, ½ lb. ham, 6 slices each American & Swiss [cheese] & ½ dozen eggs fried ... GOOD LUCK!!!" Cost: $24.50, or nothing if you could eat it all.

I went for the health food: chili with onions and cheese, and a blackberry milkshake. ◆

Cook's Box — Vegan

S. MAKAI ANDREWS

Your Story

You've started getting a weekly produce box delivered to your apartment to make sure you always eat something. You started cooking young, learning how to scramble eggs long before you knew your multiplication tables. It always came pretty easily to you, and you liked the physicality of it. Here are the ingredients; here is what you do with them; here is what they will become.

Some people who are obsessed with food as a kid become chefs. Others develop eating disorders. You found yourself somewhere in between, a stunted eating disorder and a quiet interest in food.

Featured Ingredient: Olive Oil

This week the thing that scares you most is olive oil. Last week it was white flour, a fear that bubbled up so fast you almost slapped the bagel out of your own hand when you realized what you were doing. But not this week. This week it's oil.

You can find cheap olive oil, cut with vegetable oil or the likes of Crisco, or you can find the nice ones, like you've received in your box here today. This is how you know it's high quality: pop off the lid and take a deep, sharp inhale. Is it peppery? Bright, earthy? Does it remind you of the color green? If so, you're on the right track.

This bottle will probably last you the next couple months. You never add enough oil to your cooking. Instead, you char the bottoms of pans with a hiss of cold broccoli against the searing surface. There's no fat source for the vegetables to soak and fry in, so instead it goes straight from fresh to burnt. Young to dead.

Pan-Roasted Root Vegetables: Your "I Can Eat Normally" Meal

Prep time: 30 minutes
Cook time: 1 hour

Start by chopping any and all root vegetables you have been leaving to rot in the back of your vegetable drawer: that squash you already know you'll hate, those sweet potatoes with little warts on them, and the onions on the back shelf that are somehow still growing more ugly little sprouts. This week you're tossing in cauliflower too, because for whatever reason you've ended up with a pound of the stuff, hidden behind the orange juice. Rinse the dirt off everything.

Someone will tell you later that squash isn't a root vegetable. Question your ability to cook anything at all.

Peel any skins that you think will be too thick to roast, the densest ones with the highest calorie content. Chop them up into small, bite-size pieces that will enable you to look like you're eating more than you really are. Put everything on a sheet pan with the oven set to 375°. Drizzle the pan with that olive oil that terrifies you oh so much, mix in chopped onions and minced garlic until every chunk is coated in at least one of your seasonings. Add salt and pepper.

Bake for an hour, or until you see fit. You tend to take yours out right before they're about to burn.

Olive Oil Cake with Raspberry Drizzle: Your Binge Meal

Prep time: 10 minutes
Cook time: 45 minutes

Use a Bundt pan because you think all the other options are ugly. Coat the pan with nonstick cooking spray, or a vegan nut-butter if you're feeling ballsy. Whisk together the vegan buttermilk that makes you want to gag and set it aside so you can ruminate. Add all the calories: cups of sugar and flour and salt. Pour everything in the pan, trying to stop yourself from counting calories as the batter slops from one vessel to the other.

Set your oven to 350° and bake for 45 minutes, during which time you can either compulsively panic-exercise to try to burn off some of the calories you're about to consume or give in to your vices and shove handfuls of cereal and trail mix into your gaping mouth until the cake is done.

Make the raspberry drizzle; you remember how. You learned that the day your dad told you he had a new family: the recipe does, and will, remain fresh forever.

Take the cake out of the pan, pour on the drizzle, and garnish with powdered sugar. More than you need. Make it look like snowfall, like a bloody raspberry trail through a blizzard. ◆

Tiny Florets

ENID KASSNER

I'm performing surgery on a cauliflower, sectioning its massive brain into tiny florets. I've never been one to just whack off a chunk and leave the exposed edges bleak, like a strip-mined mountain. I use a paring knife to make a cone-shaped excavation of the core, and then separate as many of the florets as I want to cook.

I will never eat cauliflower raw—which is the only way my mother ever served it when I was growing up. Cauliflower and broccoli taste better cooked. End of story. If they are being served as crudités, they should be parboiled. For that matter, green beans and sugar snap peas are not tasty raw—I don't care how many people eat them this way.

But back to the cauliflower. Some five years ago my off-again/on-again boyfriend and I were preparing dinner in his kitchen. As we scrutinized the contents of his refrigerator, he said, "Why don't we have tiny florets of cauliflower?" He suggested how we prepare them, but I now forget whether it was with curry spices or tahini.

Tiny florets. The phrase touched me, tenderly, sweetly. He—an egregious violator of whole cauliflower heads, whacking into them and leaving the edges to gray in the fridge—he could yearn for the tiny floret.

I suppose I felt that he often sliced into my tender feelings with the careless disregard shown his heads of cauliflower. If he treated a cauliflower this way, why would I expect more delicate attention to my feelings?

Nevertheless, I remember making the tiny florets, removing even the tender stems, so that we could feast on only the most delicious part of the cauliflower, each tiny floret's contours exposed and bathed in seasoning.

Ever since that evening, I have looked at a cauliflower as something composed, not just of florets, but of *tiny* florets. Now when I operate on a head, I first remove the core. But then, each large floret receives the same surgical approach. I make a conical incision at the base of the large floret, removing its stem and core. From there, I separate the larger floret into tiny florets. I do not discard the stems. I cook them along with the tiny florets. If I'm having guests, however, I generally separate out the stems for my own consumption, leaving the best for company.

Those who dine at my home might examine their food closely to evaluate where they rank. If I'm in love, each small act of food preparation is devotional. I will spend loving minutes carefully separating fresh herbs from their stems—a painstaking and tedious process. If I'm rushed, or angry, or cooking out of obligation, I might chop the herbs stems and all—to hell with it. If I'm cooking just for me, I suppose it depends on how nurturing I want to be to myself. But I've never understood people who live alone and don't cook saying, "I don't want to cook just for myself." Who better to cook for?

When lives are full and busy with work, children, parents, pets, extra-curricular activities, and obligations, the realities of food preparation may be burdensome. Perhaps a packet of frozen vegetables is tossed into the microwave as the cook shrugs her (or his) shoulders and thinks—at least I'm making a vegetable and not serving fast food.

But preparing delicious food has always been a priority for me. I enjoy the meditation of chopping my vegetables just so, squeezing the excess liquid out of blocks of tofu, washing rice and discarding the cloudy water at least three times, removing cloves of garlic from their papery husks, grinding pepper, squeezing lemons, and sprinkling salt.

I fill softened rice paper wraps with lettuce, fried tofu, cucumber, and cilantro, enjoying the miniature hands of the cilantro leaves peeking through the translucent wrapper as I dip the roll into peanut sauce seasoned with chile, lime, hoisin, sesame oil, garlic, and a hint of sugar. I chop fresh mint, vine-ripened tomatoes, cucumbers, and scallions to mix with wheat, lemon juice, olive oil, salt, and pepper for tabbouleh. I cook chickpeas in the pressure cooker and flavor them with fennel, coriander, peaches, chiles, ground almonds, and lemon juice.

But, for versatility, it's hard to beat the cauliflower, which yields willingly to Indian, Spanish, Italian, or Lebanese cuisine. And, even just for me, regardless of whether I'm off-again or on-again with my boyfriend, I craft it into tiny florets, sculpted with care, consumed with pleasure. ◆

Scab Eaters Anonymous

KATHRYN FITZPATRICK

Gabby had a heated swimming pool in her backyard, so every year from third grade through middle school she threw a Halloween party underwater. Kids jumped in the pool fully costumed and went home with rashes where the Lycra rubbed their skin wrong.

Gabby's mom always had the best snacks: Cheetos Puffs or those M&M's cookies you scoop out of a plastic tub, Bagel Bites and mini cheeseburgers and one-pound bags of kettle corn. Gabby's family used money in a way that mine didn't; they had granite countertops and a backsplash in their kitchen, while our kitchen hadn't been remodeled since 1966. The only time I felt rich was when my parents took me out for my birthday to Carmen Anthony's Fish House, where my mom waitressed, and I ordered crème brûlée on employee discount.

My mom always said you could tell the quality of a restaurant by the quality of their crème brûlée, and I don't know if this is true, but I know that I loved everything about it. The glorified pudding. The way you could smash through the top like cracked ice, the way it got caught in your teeth for the next hour. Sometimes it would come burnt, or too salty, or the custard might have too many lumps in it, but it always tasted expensive, always the dessert of choice for people with more money than us.

One year at Gabby's party we played spin the bottle and truth or dare after her parents were asleep. We were eleven or we were twelve, or maybe thirteen, at the cusp of adolescence when it's still cool to play flip cup with Dr Pepper.

"Truth or dare," Gabby said. And she looked at Mike with his preteen acne, ready to kiss him, full braces, because he was almost six feet tall.

"Truth," he said.

Gabby sighed. "What's the most embarrassing thing you've done?"

"I dunno. Pissed myself?"

The girls giggled. My turn.

"Truth or dare?"

I said dare, trying to seem cooler than I was. Without makeup or a bra or hair combed into a perfect braid (or combed at all), I didn't belong at this party. But Gabby's parents were friends with my parents, and I snatched up the pity invite year after year, sat on the side of the pool, anticipated invitations to hang out that never came.

"OK, I dare you to eat your scab."

Here's the thing: I always ate my scabs. If I fell on the sidewalk and scraped my knee, I'd wait days for it to form, peel it open, press it until blood filled the cracks, tear it, swallow. I liked the destruction of it. I liked when my mom yelled at me to stop. I also liked the way scabs tasted. I rarely went outside, so a scab was a special occasion kind of occurrence, like a fancy dessert in a restaurant I couldn't afford.

I pulled the scab from my elbow and let it soak on my tongue like a Werther's Original: wait, breathe, dissolve.

The other kids looked on, shocked.

"Are you kidding?" someone said. "That went down way easy."

Frantic, I tried to resolve my sin, gagging and choking, squeezing out tears.

"No way," said Gabby. "No way."

It was too late. The group recognized my transgression and held onto it. In the pool, when someone lost a Band-Aid, someone shouted for me to eat that, too.

The shame hit hard, like the shame of living in a house without a Jacuzzi tub or a picket fence or a Roomba, the scab in my gut, heavier than crème brûlée. ◆

Driving William Stafford

RICHARD ROBBINS

The only thing we talked about was bread. How to keep the crust from splitting in the oven's heat. How to keep the rise from falling. What the kneading did for the hands.

It was 3 a.m., as dark as early morning gets, and 26° below. I looked it up. At least once per mile, the right side of the car blew onto the shoulder, and I had to ease us back over black ice into our lane. There was no other traffic. I still wonder how hard the wind gusted—that's what I remember most—but I can't find the record. Let's be generous and say twenty miles per hour, which made for a wind chill of –55°. With snow depth at 18 inches (I looked it up), a good amount of snow was blowing around too. Stafford's flight left Minneapolis at 6:15 a.m. He needed to be at Olivet College in Michigan that afternoon.

He had recently discovered sprouted wheat bread. The recipe required a few days of forethought: the wheat berries soaking out of daylight, then the twice-daily rinsing until they sprouted and the tiniest roots had begun to form. He promised it would be nutty and sweet if I tried making some.

"You won't be disappointed."

Nine months before, I had invited him to Mankato to talk to us and read from his work. Stafford agreed to all parts of the suggested program. I asked him what he charged.

"Be generous if you think of including me," he wrote back. "I don't know what to say about my value ..."

We might have talked about the new poems he read the night before, about Cannon Beach or Multnomah Trail in Oregon, about Richard Hugo or David Wagoner or Madeline DeFrees, about the other World War II conscientious objectors. But he seemed to want to keep the conversation focused, detail-oriented. It was 3 a.m. Neither of us even imagined owning a cell phone in 1988. There was no other traffic. If we'd gone in the ditch, we might have frozen to death.

You think about someone whose work you particularly admire, about someone whose larger life has visible benchmarks you'd like, as a fellow artist, to remember. You think about that person and expect you'd take any advantage a moment together would offer you. By the time you are driving back to the airport, though, you have asked all the writerly questions during a radio interview. You have had another chance, with others, at a craft talk. What was missing was the perfect moment to ask the perfect question about just you, something that would re-chart your course for the foreseeable future. But by then you were almost friends, and to press such things would have been aggressive and rude. Stafford wanted to talk about bread.

Three years later, I invited him back to Mankato.

"Another encounter there is an enticing prospect," he wrote back, "but something drastic has happened—I got a big grant and have to abjure engagements for a while to perform my writing and be grateful! Don't forget me, please. I'll recover from the grant one of these days ..."

The sourdough starter my wife and I had made was going on ten years old. I preferred oat flakes sprinkled on the dough to seeds or an egg wash. Stafford and I agreed about pans. About unbleached, of course, over bleached. Stoneground over any other. We agreed about when, if, and with what kind of blade to make slashes in the risen dough. Molasses over sugar. Honey over molasses. We agreed God could not improve upon buttered toast.

I could just see the road. ◆

Death by Corn Candy

HOPE NISLY

All her life, Colleen had a fondness for a conflation of food and ritual: fondue on New Year's Eve, cinnamon rolls every Sunday morning, chocolate for all celebrations, a cup of dark roast coffee shared with friends just because. Normally frugal to a fault, she spared no cost for the food and drink she shared with others.

At our last Thanksgiving meal together, when it was difficult for her to stand up for more than five minutes at a time, she held on long enough to prepare the turkey with her husband's assistance. She placed herbs and garlic under the skin, then filled it with a special sausage and mushroom stuffing. The rest of us assembled the remainder of the feast: the vegetarian offerings, several sides, and the pumpkin and pecan pies. We did not do it alone, however. She directed our efforts with the precision of a choreographer. She sent her brother out for the best wine. We roasted the brussels sprouts to her exact specifications and assembled a grated carrot salad from her grandmother's vintage family recipe that had never been written down. She supervised the bread baking with her own special recipe; we did not stop kneading until she said "enough."

We knew we would never share another Thanksgiving meal, but we did not know that it would be our last supper, our final breaking of bread.

A few weeks later, just before emergency tracheotomy surgery that would keep the cancer cells from suffocating her, we talked on the phone. Knowing that after the surgery she would not be able to speak or swallow, we savored the details of our Thanksgiving gathering while I absorbed the last time I would hear her voice, certainly for months, possibly forever. She recounted in full our Thanksgiving weekend together, how we drove into the mountains, how the sunshine of the late November day had been so welcome after the gray and rainy days of the fall. How the feast gave her such joy, coming in that brief interlude between her bout of chemo-induced thrush and her pre-Christmas tracheotomy.

At the end of our conversation Colleen added wistfully, "And to think that our Thanksgiving fondue was the last fondue I'll ever share with you." A family tradition on New Year's Eve, we had opted for a pre-Thanksgiving fondue, as if we knew it would be our last chance. It was this thought, the sudden assertion that we would never share another fondue, that stopped us both in our reverie, crushed by the recognition of the statement's meaning.

Post-surgery she endured her tube feedings, each one preceded by a careful inspection by the hospice nurse of the contents of her stomach. Nutrients without flavor; calories without joy. Her brother, Doug, stood by her bed, sipping on a cup of espresso when she reached for him, pointing to the packages of sponges on her bedside table. She wrote *"taste"* on the whiteboard, now her only means of communication. He picked up the small sponge on a stick, the one we used to keep her mouth moist. Like a priest offering communion, he dipped it solemnly into the coffee and held it out to her. Her tongue glided over the sponge, her expression revealing a momentary spark of joy.

She sent us off to lunch, facetiously giving us whiteboard instructions to "get the best the hospital cafeteria offers." If she could not eat, she would partake of vicariously, even if it didn't meet her usual standards. When we got back to the room Doug held a cup of corn candy, the only "dessert" he could find that sounded better than the cafeteria's selections of gelatin and pudding. She pointed and wrote *"what is it?"* He held out a piece, which she took and licked carefully.

She smiled languidly, scribbled *"death by corn candy"* on the board, then closed her eyes to rest again. ◆

Hunger

RITA CIRESI

At school the brown clock says Seth Thomas. But you wish Seth would say ten o'clock. Ten is when the janitor brings in the milk crate.

You don't give a *fongool* for the milk. You've got your eye on Miss Teacher's Honey Maid graham cracker box. You can't wait until she pulls out a thick brick of graham crackers, breaks each cracker in two, and gives you a half that's scored down the middle.

You can either eat your half-cracker whole or you can break it into two separate pieces. You bust yours in two because that way it seems like you got more.

After the last bite dissolves in your mouth you do the same as all the rest of the first graders: lick your finger and pick up every single crumb from the dirty wooden desk, then lick your finger again.

Miss Teacher says this is bad manners.

So is asking for seconds. So you don't.

Between the time Seth Thomas ticks from ten to twelve o'clock, you think about the rumor going around school that you'll get a whole graham cracker instead of just half when you reach second grade.

At noon you walk home, bony knees knocking against each other and stomach rumbling. You wonder what Ma's got for lunch. You dream about a *legna*—a whole loaf of 'talian bread—stuffed with fat-pocked salami and thick chunks of provolone. But most of the time Ma spreads a thin coat of Jif peanut butter on a slice of Sunbeam bread. She calls these open-faced sandwiches, which is a fancy way of saying she only has to use one slice.

In winter Ma makes white rice with a teaspoon of milk and a sprinkle of sugar on top. Some days there's no milk. Other days, no sugar.

On TV, ladies go next door to borrow a cup of sugar. Ma doesn't.

Back at school you keep your eyes on Seth Thomas until his hands reach two o'clock. Two means Art. Art class is the best class. When the teacher isn't looking, you can eat the paste and suck on the clay.

After school you follow the fat girls home. The fat girls really got to eat. At their house chocolate milk comes out chocolate straight from the carton. Here you can *mangiar'* six Oreos instead of one. Nobody's counting.

Fat Donna has all the Oreos she wants to eat at home. But on the walk back she still stops at Bruno's Market and buys twin packs of Ding Dongs and Ring Dings. Sometimes she gives you a ding or a dong. The rest of the time you watch her eat both.

You set the table with forks and spoons. Never knives. Knives are for Sunday supper, when sometimes there's meat inside the macaroni. Other times, not.

You never use plates. You always eat from bowls. Like this:
Colazione: bowl of cereal.
Pranzo: bowl of rice.
Cena: bowl of macaroni.

In the dark, before you fall asleep, you think about the picture books you've read at school, where the bowls never run out of soup and the pasta pot keeps growing spaghetti. ◆

Proof of the Pudding

TERRI ELDERS

My spouse, Ken, spotted the banana pudding mix I'd set on the kitchen counter. "No pudding in any guise," he warned me.

"Oh, I thought I'd mash these soft bananas and stir them into that mix. You like banana cream pie."

"Make banana bread instead. I don't do pudding."

I added pudding to a list that already included cabbage, sweet potatoes, and deviled eggs. But I regretted Ken's refusal to taste the down-home dishes Grandma had taught me to cook, the nostalgic nibbles I dearly loved. He'd even declined fried zucchini.

This was the same man who'd bragged he'd savored snails in garlic sauce, purchased from a street vendor next to the Eiffel Tower. He'd lamented that he couldn't find quark, a kind of yogurt cheese he'd favored when he'd lived in Germany. And Ken never pushed away any kind of fried meat.

A devotee of Miguel de Cervantes, Ken collected Don Quixote paintings and images. He'd complained about his hero's diet, described in the opening pages of Cervantes's seventeenth-century Spanish novel as sparse, monotonous and unpalatable.

"If Quixote and I hung out, I'd insist he try a chicken-fried steak," Ken said. "That would help fatten him up."

I disliked having to toss out a dish that didn't please his palate. Ken knew I hated to throw food away. My years in the Peace Corps had taught me it's unethical to waste food.

One spring as we weeded the front yard, I'd held aloft a dandelion, lamenting that I couldn't remember how Grandma had prepared her "mess o' greens."

"She wilted the dandelion leaves in bacon grease, and added onion and garlic," I began, dreamily recalling the aroma. "I think she added a dash of vinegar. Or maybe it was pepper sauce."

"It would be a mess, all right," Ken had retorted, yanking the weeds from my hand and tossing them into the wheelbarrow.

I usually went along, but when it came to bread, I balked. I believed that letting bread grow moldy amounted to blasphemy. Bread, Grandma taught me, was the staff of life. Every crumb had value. Stale loaves could transform into croutons to sprinkle on French onion soup, or crumbs to pad out meat loaf, or cubes to stir into stewed tomatoes.

One morning I noticed that some of the apples I'd stored in our pantry when they'd ripened on our trees the past autumn had begun to look dehydrated. I also saw we had half a loaf of more-than-a-day-old French bread.

I thumbed through my recipes and found Grandma's instructions for apple bread pudding. *Aha!* Maybe I'd claim it was Brown Betty. Grandma made that, too, but it didn't contain milk and eggs. Ken wouldn't know the difference. After all, in *Don Quixote* Miguel de Cervantes had immortalized the adage (in one translation, anyway), "The proof of the pudding is in the eating."

Sometimes Grandma served her bread pudding with a sauce, either vanilla or caramel, but since Ken scrunched up his face at syrupy toppings, I'd garnish with whipped cream, which he loved.

"Ready for dessert, honey? I baked something this afternoon."

Ken favored me with his lopsided smile. "What's it called?"

I scooped a couple of servings into custard cups. I have difficulty telling even a little white lie without turning crimson, so I averted my face. I squirted whipped cream, cooking up an evasion.

"Oh, it's something Grandma used to bake. It's an old-fashioned dish, like a Brown Betty with apples."

Ken ate every bite. "It's paradisiacal," he said. "I'll take seconds. What's it called again? How do you make it??"

I bit my lip and handed him Grandma's recipe card.

"Bread pudding?" Ken sputtered. "I thought you said it was Brown Betty."

"Hmmm. I must have pulled out the wrong recipe. Still want seconds? It's uh, pudding. That you don't do in any guise."

Ken grinned and handed me his bowl. "Guess I can't say *that* anymore."

There's more than one way to skin a cat, I've heard. Wait ... did Miguel de Cervantes say that? No ... I think it was Grandma. ◆

Fast Food

JESSE WATERS

The snow-white husky under the pew in the foyer is watching the humans at the butcher block table in the middle of the kitchen. The father in the suede suit coat has been back from his job twenty-two minutes and forty-eight seconds, and is eating eleven peanuts cracked open from their shells, three smears of wine cheese across three wheat crackers, and one apple slice. But his is a voracious appetite.

"How about some McDonald's?" he says.

My stomach buckles: The most popular kid on the block, Cross, is staying for dinner.

The four of us pack into the family car, a mid-size luxury diesel.

Dad thinks his offer of McDonald's means grace, and benevolence, and providence. Jews don't usually eat fast food. Or at least we didn't.

We putter away from the house. Eleven minutes, twenty-nine seconds, and 7.34 miles later, our car pulls into the drive-through. The white bag comes into the car. My hell begins.

I lean forward over the seats to reach for a few hot fries. Horking a few perfect drive-through fries in the car is something everyone on the planet does, everyone except the parents in this vehicle. But I had to at least try and secure that lode for Cross and myself. Cross was the kid every other eleven-year-old wanted to be friends with.

I wanted to be him: He had Atari first, and cable TV first, perfectly feathered light auburn hair parted in the middle, and his father let him work out with him on free weights, and his house was the one on the corner with the big yard just across from the cement ball courts, his front door maybe ten yards from the regular stopping point of the ice cream truck.

But my mother crushes the top of the bag closed. "Just wait till we get home." No fries, no sips of soda—nothing more than delicious bag-air filling the car with silent want. No one speaks. The car smells like fried potatoes, yet so unlike latkes.

Inside the house, the bag and my parents move to that butcher block table. Cross and I head for the dining room. We sit down.

"What're your parents doing?" Cross whispers.

The two of us watch from our seats as an odd triage begins in the kitchen. Four plates emerge from their cabinet place, and the two burgers, a Quarter Pounder, and a Filet O' Fish are placed one on each plate at eleven o'clock. Fries come out of their bags between two and four o'clock. Four glasses come fresh and clean from the dishwasher, mouths wide as they wait to swallow the root beer and clear Sprite now being transferred from wax paper cup to glass. With plates in hands, my parents walk into the dining room, serve, and sit down.

There are parsley sprigs on each plate.

Cross and I wolf down our meals, and ten minutes later, outside in the late-winter, street-lit dusk, bouncing a basketball around, I try to joke about what bizarre parents I have.

"That's cool," he says, "it makes sense. My dad says your folks are kikes. You even sort of look like Ronald McDonald."

I have no idea what any of that is, or means. *Kike*—man! It bites like a dark fang. *My parents, those fucking Kikes*, I think to myself, and Cross and I run down the hardtack white of the sidewalks alongside our D.C. suburb houses to where the block kids are waiting, and I have something to tell them. ◆

The Thanksgiving Bird

MIRA MARTIN-PARKER

My dad had a very specific technique for cooking our Thanksgiving turkey, inspired by George Ohsawa, the founder of the macrobiotic diet my parents followed religiously when I was young. This method involved brining the turkey overnight in a mixture of water, garlic, cracked pepper, and tamari. Using a basting brush, Dad would wake up dutifully every hour the night before and carefully baste the top of the turkey with his tamari brine. The next day he'd stuff the bird with roasted brown rice stuffing (another recipe inspired by George Ohsawa), carefully wrap it in miles of heavy-duty aluminum foil, place it in the oven on a low flame, and cook it for the entire day—insisting that this slow cooking made the meat extra-tender.

I don't have any memories of the excellence of my dad's turkey. But I do have memories of him being so grumpy from staying up all night basting the thing that he could barely make it through the "Oh Thou the Sustainer" Sufi grace* without yelling at one of us kids and ruining the meal. Afterward, he'd sit silently scowling down at his plate, letting everyone know he was in one of his dangerous moods (*Shhh, keep quiet, don't piss off Dad*). It was a horribly depressing scene, and in my opinion, any benefits gained from basting the turkey every hour the night before were more than lost in the resulting damage done to our holiday festivities.

In contrast, my mother was considerably more lighthearted when she prepared Thanksgiving dinner. I don't recall her turkey cooking technique, but I do remember the two of us laughing in the kitchen as she told me stories about my Italian-Irish-Portuguese grandmother routinely tossing the Thanksgiving turkey out the window in a fit of rage. One year she recalled her entire family eating frozen dinners because Grandmother's bird had gone out the window and was unsalvageable. Thankfully Mother never tossed our turkey, but I do remember her once chucking a stuffed bell pepper at her boyfriend. Fortunately he ducked, and it hit the wall. For weeks we were sweeping up bits of brown rice from the dining room floor.

In spite of my bumpy family history, Thanksgiving is still one of my favorite holidays. And because I love it so much, I do everything in my power to make sure no grumpiness or drama takes place.

Over the years I've managed to create a turkey recipe that's relatively trouble free—even though it does involve a tamari marinade, which results in the crunchiest, most flavorful skin you've ever tasted. My stuffing is a modified version of my dad's macro brown rice recipe, only I add wild rice, apples, and fresh herbs for cheer. My mashed potatoes are vegan to avoid the American wide-ass spread, and are every bit as yummy as the traditional version. And my gravy—well, let's just say the tamari from the turkey does something magical to it. My husband bakes a divine apple pie and is also in charge of roasting the bird, and I usually take over with the usual unnecessary vegetable sides. In our over twenty years together, no turkey has been tossed in our household, nor has our son had to put up with grumpy, sullen parents at the table. Like I said, Thanksgiving is my favorite holiday, and I do my best to keep it happy.

Sufi grace: Oh thou the sustainer of our bodies, hearts, and souls, bless all that we receive in thankfulness. Until the very end, Jai Baba. ◆

Stalemate

KRISTINA MORICONI

Walking home every day from elementary school at lunch, I stopped to pour my carton of whole milk down a sewer drain along the way.

At the beginning of the school year, I'd asked my mother if I could sign up for chocolate milk, but she said no and sent in the form for white milk instead.

And, so, our battle for control began.

The milk, a preamble.

The conflict at our kitchen table would be far worse. Five o'clock, every night. Neither of us willing to compromise.

It started small: lima beans. At least once a week. It was a textural thing for me. They were chalky. And, by the time my mother had taken them from a bag in the freezer to the table, they'd been purged of any taste they might've once had.

It shifted to liver and onions.

Then, almost daily, to some kind of bloody meat. Ropey tendons and ribbons of fat running through each slab. Roast beef. Lamb. Tenderloin.

Steak was my father's favorite. Top round. Bottom round. Flap. Skirt. Strip. Flank. Rib-eye. London broil. T-bone.

It didn't matter how small I cut them up. I chewed and chewed, but the pieces of meat never seemed to get any smaller. As often as possible, when my mother wasn't looking, whatever had been in my mouth ended up in the napkin on my lap.

I wasn't allowed to leave the table until I finished *everything on my plate.* Meat was expensive, my father reminded me. There were starving children in the world, my mother proclaimed. Often.

It was the late seventies. I don't know how much information was out there about the risks of creating disordered behavior in your children. But I do know those hours at that kitchen table, alone, sometimes long after dark, willing myself not to eat, set the stage for a lifetime of struggle.

I learned then—and I learned well—how to tame the hunger in my belly. To fall asleep listening to the grumble.

My mother got our week's worth of meat from the local butcher. I went with her.

I had never seen my mother giddy before, but she looked and sounded like a young schoolgirl around this man behind the counter. She called him by his first name—Heinz. He spoke with a thick German accent my mother once told me she loved listening to. And she always bought whatever *cut*-of-this or *fillet*-of-that he recommended to her.

I didn't know exactly what flirting was back then, but I'm sure now my mother had been doing exactly that with Heinz the butcher.

She always left that market smiling, seeming a little lighter, our bags weighed down by meat wrapped neatly in brown paper, tied up with white string.

Years later, near the end of my mother's life, she moved into an assisted living community. She was happy to have someone cook for her.

I didn't realize how much she'd never actually enjoyed cooking until my father died and she stopped making meals, unless they were frozen and came from a box.

Once she moved into the Manor, she quickly got used to three meals a day being prepared for her. And she quickly became picky. Demanding. Sometimes, almost combative, about what it was she would and would not eat.

She made a list. Chicken: boiled only, unseasoned. Rice: white, over-cooked. Baked potato: plain, preferably twice-baked. Vegetables: steamed, but not asparagus or brussels sprouts.

Of course, I thought back to my childhood and our kitchen table. To the hours I'd spent fretting over foods I didn't want to eat. I never said anything to my mother, though. There was no point.

I lifted her knife and fork to slice the dry, bland chicken breast on her plate into small pieces, exactly how she wanted them.

For me, by now a vegetarian for decades, this was an act of love.

She never thanked me. But that was my mother. Thanking me would have been an acknowledgement of need and that would've meant, for her, giving up whatever illusion of control she still desperately clung to.

Before she began stabbing her fork into the perfect cubes of chicken, I removed the white linen napkin the dining staff had fan-folded and placed inside her wine glass. As it unfurled in the air, I couldn't help but think of that moment as a gesture of surrender.

I set the napkin in her lap and smiled. ◆

For the Love of Pie

JOHN GIFFORD

In the winter of 1990 I was a young Marine stationed in Saudi Arabia in support of Operation Desert Shield. At a time before e-mail and the Internet, our lifeline to friends and family back home was the mail we sent and received. I can still remember the excitement and anticipation of assembling for mail call.

One evening I heard the mail sergeant call my name and I walked up to take my letter, but he handed me instead a large box addressed from my grandmother back home in Oklahoma. One of the great hardships of the war for me was the absence of my grandmother's cooking—her skillet-fried chicken and okra, homemade cornbread, and most of all, her desserts. But on this evening I was about to take a gastronomic journey home, for I opened the box to find two dozen of my grandmother's apricot fried pies.

Having noticed my mail, a buddy from New York approached and asked what I'd received. I couldn't answer him; my mouth was full of apricots. So I just offered him a pie.

"These are awesome!" he said. "What are they?"

He had to wait a few moments for an answer, but eventually I explained. And as insurance, I offered him another pie to keep quiet. After all, my supply of this Southern staple was finite and I was pretty sure none of the other Marines had any fried pies there in camp.

Thereafter, once a day for the next three weeks, I indulged my palate and returned home to my grandmother's kitchen, if only for a few sweet bites at a time.

Some of my earliest recollections involve my grandmother's pies and especially her sweet, flaky crust, which she could turn out from memory. As she had been baking pies since before the Great Depression, I suppose there was no way she could forget how to create these delights. And it didn't matter which basic ingredients you gave her, she always knew what to do with them. She would have baffled the judges on today's television cooking challenges.

I remember coming across a persimmon tree once while out hiking in the woods. It was autumn and the fruit was soft and sweet, so I picked a few dozen and brought them to Grandma. The next day I walked into her kitchen to find a persimmon pie waiting for me.

As I aged, my love of pies never waned. Blueberry, cherry, pecan, or pumpkin—you name it and I've eaten it. In fact, I had pies in place of a groom's cake at my wedding. Being so busy that evening, I didn't get a bite, though our guests raved about them.

I once had a dog that loved pie almost as much as I. One afternoon I placed a steaming chocolate cream on the counter to cool before leaving the house to run an errand. My mouth watered just thinking about that pie, and I resolved to have a piece the moment I returned. But when I walked back into the house, something was strange. The pie's pretty cream topping, its smooth chocolate filling, were gone. All that remained was a greasy-looking crust that more closely resembled a child's finger painting than a pie. (My grandmother would have said it looked like chickens had been scratching around in it.) I couldn't understand what had happened until I looked down and noticed Ollie, my wheaten terrier, watching me from the corner. He was licking his mouth.

Like Ollie, I'll eat most any pie you place in front of me. But when asked about my favorite, I always say that I have only two: hot and cold. ◆

Kitchen Dalliances

MARILYN LEVINE

I am alone now. Not just living alone, but *being* alone. I'm not fighting it: I feel like a stone dug into the sand of a shallow ocean shore, characterologically motionless—but for the velocity of the breaking tide, which is itself controlled by the gravitational whimsy of the sun and the moon. I am here, not seeking, not yearning to go anywhere or be anything but what, or who, I am.

But life is nothing if not a paradox: Right after my sorrowful divorce, I began experimenting with ways to transcend the inertness of my heart—with an incongruous blast to my senses. I was reminded how much I love to touch food. I like to disrobe it, to turn it on (and off). Sometimes I get a new relationship off to a bad start by combining, say, a musky cauliflower with a whole package of heirloom French Chantenay carrots in a chicken stew—as it turns out, these two have no business being together in the same universe. But I do get excited trying, which is the whole point of straying from convention in the first place, isn't it? And there are times I feel an extraordinary rush of well-being from my culinary dalliances, as when I turn out unmistakably dazzling dishes from nothing but the shy, overlooked remnants in my cabinets and vegetable bins. I never work from recipes. That's my rule. I just look around and start cutting things up, never assuming that if I'm boiling pasta on one burner, then I must be cooking tomato sauce on the other. You can never be entirely certain what a mound of steaming penne wants on top of it until you open yourself up to all the possibilities.

And this is precisely my pleasure: the whole question of what's below and what's on top seems a lot more enthralling in the realm of food preparation than in my bedroom. I find myself compelled to being open to unimaginable possibilities—all requiring a mental and physical *rythme ralenti*, as the French say, a certain slowed-down pace, even a suspension of expectation. And so it is when I hold a pale, succulent bok choy in the palm of my hand. Time seems to stand still. A pocket of warm air surrounds me as I ponder whether to make vertical or horizontal slices and then sauté my tender pieces

in virgin olive oil, just long enough to infuse a civility into their rawness without eradicating their innocence; or, to spare the upright, perky form, cutting
only its blunt lower end to release the dozen or so small fronds attached to it.
And then there's the whole question of how to make sure this lovely Eastern
charmer is seen in her best light—starkly alone on a white platter, or in the
gay company of julienned carrots and beet slivers piled together in a volup-
tuous glass bowl? Such decisions cannot, as I said, be rushed.

Back in the day, I often worried that my secret love of chopping would be
seen for what it was—a brief, even poignant relationship with the mystery of
the mundane and the sensual, for the sake of my own fragile equilibrium. As
I said, now I am alone, now I am experiencing the solitary joy of finding eter-
nity in a smattering of onions, glory in the trimming of a Jerusalem artichoke.
When I reach into the refrigerator and pull out a few umbelliferous greens, I
am struck by the realization that I no longer have to deal with the unsavory
taste of a dying marriage. I cook to remember who I am, to feel and taste
and listen to the sounds of my own slicing, my own yearning. This is the same
kind of total absorption that enveloped me when I gave birth to our first child.
They called it natural delivery, and now I know why: everything around me
in the birthing room—bodies, noises, smells, movements—slid away into the
recesses of my consciousness, and everything inside of me came forward, as
if the real and the dream world had switched places. In only a slightly less
profound way, cooking is my natural delivery from emotional entropy. I gaze
on a counter littered with parsley, ripe roma tomatoes, arugula, and lemons,
and I am struck by all the destinies waiting to be discovered. I contemplate a
glass jar filled with pine nuts, a burlap bag of basmati rice, an unruly sprig
of lemon thyme, and I am certain that how, and if, these disparate elements
can relate to one another will become clear to me if only I can give them an
occasion for being on the same countertop together. I'll know before I know,
combine these separate food groups before I know why, or where it will all
lead. By doing what seems right, I'll figure out what is right, and not right.
That's the only way. ◆

Translations

ELIZABETH DANEK

A sea breeze cools Pokrovnik, a small village outside Šibenik, Croatia, where I visit my husband's family. A dusty Skoda bobbles along the dirt road and rustling olive tree leaves are the only audible sounds. Our children are browned by the Adriatic sun, exhausted, saliva at their chins. Inside the house, fast asleep, are *Baba* Šima, Ivan's grandmother, ninety; his aunt, *Teta* Zorka, and her husband, *Tetak* Niko, farmers in their mid-sixties.

We make our way to the kitchen to make tea, and Zorka pops up from a red couch, a common Eastern European guest bed the host takes.

"Jesteli jeli?" she asks. Had we eaten?

In every house and *gostionica* we encountered, I want to say. Roast lamb, prosciutto, *ajvar*, *burek*. Another day it was octopus and calamari. We drank shots of *rakija* and liters of red wine. And always sipped thick, velvety coffee. I am food weary. But that does not deter Zorka from preparing one more meal—at midnight—*so we can sleep*. My husband reminds me: Declining food will offend his favorite aunt.

"Samo malo," he says. Just a little, he guarantees.

Dense aromas fill the kitchen. My husband joins Niko in the *konoba*, a separate room kept cool to store dangling hams, cheese, corn, and looming in the dark, enormous barrels full of red wine.

Zorka whisks eggs while Baba sets the table. Antonio, a year old, sleeps on the couch, while Mario, age five, sits with me.

"Malo mozga?" *Teta* Zorka asks, her gray hair braid unraveling at her crown.

The name is familiar. Like *Mozak*. But it is late and all our languages scramble. *Mozak* escapes me. Is that eel? I ask.

I swore I would never ask my children to translate, but after learning German, my childhood Croatian escapes me. Baba tells me again that she can count in German. *Bis siebzehn.* "I baked seventeen loaves of bread for the Germans—in one day." In a year, she will witness another war.

Mozak? I forget, Mario says. He is the worn traveler.

The men surfaface, carrying bread and jugs of wine in *damlijane,* demi-johns encased in straw. *Tetak* Niko drinks from a stainless steel measuring cup. *Zivili!* To us! Mario asks for *malo čaj*—a little tea—in both languages and the congregation sighs. Baba rests against her crutch, mesmerized.

"Just a bite then we can sleep," I say and ready a forkful of eggs and sautéed meat; strips of onion and tomato gleam in their juices. No one would serve eel with eggs.

"*I remember now,*" Mario announces.

My fork is poised to feed him, but he declines. He wants to tell me something. I take the mouthful instead; Zorka beams. The braised meat with eggs and herbs soothes me. Chamomile flowers steep in a tall pot and now, I know, we will sleep.

Mario has it: "*Teta* says if we eat *mozak,* we'll wake up smarter in the morning. *Mozak* is b-r-a-i-n, Mama. Cow brain."

Brain. I wince.

Brrlain, Baba repeats.

Baba says I speak Croatian well; my husband says, "You must be drunk, Baba."

Well, she *understands.*

A delicacy, *Teta* Zorka says. *Manje ali sladje.* She drops two more lumps of sugar into our cups and stirs for me. These acquired tastes are also my father's—*mozak, tripica* (tripe), and *jezik* (tongue), but I never gravitated to them.

My husband scrapes the pan clean.

At dawn I go for a hike toward a distant hill. The valley below leads to the River Krka; waves of lavender, wild asparagus, and almond trees swirl across the hills. I find the dark karstic cave that hosts a spring of clear and delicious water, gulp and promise to return later with Mario. I pass shepherds in my descent.

At home, another table is set, decked high with fresh bread, ham, blood sausages, cheese, fried eggs, green onions, and tomatoes with a diameter as large as the salad plates they sit on. Zorka unfurrows a brow and smiles. My husband translates. "She was worried you walked on an empty stomach."

She collects thick, yellow *skorup,* or skin from the boiling milk, onto a hunk of homemade bread slathered with butter and sprinkles sugar over it. The children are eating pitted cherries, their hands, cheeks, and chests stained crimson. I bite the bread; melted butter drips to my plate. I sip another Turkish coffee. *Manje ali sladje,* I say. *Less but sweeter.*

Izvanredan, says Baba. *Remarkable. I told you she would get it.* ◆

We Ate When We Were Hungry

CATHERINE STRATTON

Food has changed.

In the 1960s we had a no-nonsense relationship to food—we ate when we were hungry. It may not have been to our liking but kids didn't get to choose and we had to eat everything on our plates.

"There are people starving in Africa, you know," the grownups said.

We ate like Americans. The ones with no ethnicity left. Macaroni and cheese, tuna casserole, meat loaf, hot dogs—*Oh I wish I were an Oscar Mayer weiner*—and meat cuts. Lots and lots of meat cuts. I gagged on the fat. My mother took it personally.

Italian night was best: spaghetti with chopped meat and a jar of Ragú. Chinese night was La Choy and came in a can: bamboo shoots (chewy-like sticks), bean sprouts (which nobody liked), water chestnuts, baby corn served with minute steak over Minute Rice.

We called it chop suey.

Leftover nights were frequent and still sad to contemplate.

"What's for dinner?"

"Leftovers."

Sixties food didn't age well. Even with Tupperware parties.

We drank water from the tap. The only bottled water was distilled and used for ironing. We got our vitamin C from powdered drinks—Kool-Aid and Funny Face—and fought over our favorite flavors, Injun Orange and Chinese Cherry, names they wouldn't use today. And we mixed up Tang. It looked like orange sand in a jar. It was 1968. The astronauts drank it on their way to the moon. They ate Space Food Sticks too, chewy and brown and tasting like stale Tootsie Rolls.

Our trusty TVs told us, and we believed, that Wonder Bread "helps build strong bodies twelve ways," but we didn't think to ask what those twelve ways were. Milky Way, they said, was "the good food candy bar," loaded "with so much milk it moos." They lied, but our mothers didn't know it, so we kids had it made.

Coffee was percolated in the 1960s, drunk for the jolt, not for the taste. Cheese was Velveeta, lettuce was iceberg, milk was whole, butter was margarine, vegetables were boiled, spices were sparse, and dessert came in a box: My*T*Fine pudding, Junket, Whip'n Chill and the almighty, ubiquitous, indestructible Jell-O.

Jell-O was a sixties food group. It was everywhere. Not just in our kitchen cabinet. Our neighbors' too. Stacks of it. Lined up on shelves. Easy to build a tower with. Cherry, lemon, orange, grape. Only lime? You knew you were running out.

Nobody liked lime.

The joys of the Jell-O decade required Jell-O molds. We had five copper ones: a lobster, a rooster, a wreath, a scallop shell, and a flying fish. We hung them on the wall like fine art, taking them down for short stints to make Jell-O salads and desserts with names like Jellied Peach Melba, Ring Around the Tuna and Pineapple Carrot Surprise. Concoctions de rigueur at parties and family functions.

Produce was seasonal in the 1960s. There were no ethnic food aisles. Flavored coffee was a bad idea still in the future, and cappuccino a foreign word no one could pronounce. We didn't obsess about nutrition either. Fat was fat and fiber didn't matter. Flintstones Vitamins provided everything a kid needed, pesticides were not on our radar, and "organic" described the residue found under rocks.

Food was different back then—less variety, fewer healthy options—but, because we didn't have sophisticated tastes and because we had nothing to compare it to, it didn't attract the same intense focus that it does today. We ate when we were hungry, we ate what was on our plates, and that was that.

Now, fifty years on, there are designer foods, artisanal foods, locally sourced foods and slow foods. There are vegans, paleos, pescetarians and lacto-vegetarians. Chefs are celebrities, cooking shows reign, culinary tourism is booming, and foodies worship at the altar of taste.

Food *has* changed.

And, there are still people starving in Africa … and lots of other places too. ◆

Only the Lonely

JONATHAN AMMONS

I like doing things alone. I like going to see movies by myself, I like seeing concerts solo, and I love eating alone. Don't get me wrong, a booth full of friends is one of my favorite things. There is no space I adore more than sitting at a table with a dozen people, or just a date. There is no better way to get to know a group of strangers than sitting around a dinner table with them and busting each other's balls over a home-cooked meal or over a spread of plates at some local joint.

But there is something about eating alone that I absolutely love. And I never thought of that as weird or unusual until about a year ago, when I was sitting on the patio of the Noodle Shop down on Biltmore Avenue. I had a table to myself and the Big Nasty was busking on the street. I had a table full of small plates: silver potato, steamed pork dumplings, baozi, and some kind of soup, I'm sure.

So there I am, basking in the lovely fall weather, when an old friend from college spots me as he is crossing the street. He approaches my table and gives me a hug.

"Aw, are you here by yourself?" he asks, in the type of tone people use to say *How's your mother; I heard she was ill?* or, *I heard you had to put your dog down last week; are you OK?*

And my response was, "Well, yeah!" Because to me, going out to eat by yourself is kind of a standard thing. As someone who is always around people and always out in public, a dinner by myself is a fun chance to catch up on back issues of *The Economist,* or finally dip into that book my brother gave me for Christmas four years ago. It is a sacred time where I can enjoy my food and actually give it the attention it deserves, instead of pondering my witty comeback for my date's terrible icebreaker questions.

"I really like to eat alone," said Andy Warhol once in an interview. "I want to start a chain of restaurants for other people who are like me called

Andy-Mats, 'The Restaurant for the Lonely Person.' You get your food and then you take your tray into a booth and watch television." What a fantastic idea. Unfortunately, Andy wanted to make it an Automat—you know, one of those places with the wall of trays under heat lamps where you stick in your quarter, pull down the little plastic door. and pull out a precooked hamburger or cubed steak. Which could not be a grosser idea. But the concept of the lonely man's restaurant is a great idea, I think.

In countries like South Korea, it is a cultural thing that one never eats alone. My friend Joanna lived and taught there for a while, and she would tell me about trying to go out to eat by herself. "People at the table next to you would just clear a seat and invite you to sit with them. And it was really offensive if you didn't join them. And at some places they'd just seat you with another party if you came alone!" I have heard that there is even a common greeting of *Have you eaten yet?* in place of the ubiquitous American *How are you?*

I am torn on the Korean ethic here. Whereas I would love the ability to walk into any restaurant or bar by myself and know, beyond any shadow of a doubt, that I will be introduced to someone new and have a conversation that otherwise never would have taken place, I think it might drive me a little nuts. Sometimes there is nothing better than sidling up to a bar, busting out your book, and packing away a giant burger and fries while you eavesdrop on the awkward first Match.com date at the table behind you. ◆

Oranges

CATHARINA COENEN

My mother shoves a dessert knife through skin, pushes through the small opening with her fingernail, the terminal segment of her thumb. She rips. The top of the orange splits, peel trailing a string of cream-colored vasculature from beneath the green dimple of the pedicel, the former connection of fruit to stem. Perfect nails pry under rind, tear off ragged shreds. Each rupture explodes a citrus cloud into the living room. My sister and I inhale. Sweet orange oil, trapped in *Citrus sinensis* peel, is said to be uplifting, to dispel colds, lackluster skin, and stress. I doubt my mother has read this. But her body knows.

My mother, Anna, says her very first orange glowed, a solar pinprick in a world of lead. I can see her there, at eight years old, in the city of Essen, Germany, in January 1948, after years of bombings, desperation, death. She trudges through a winter of starvation, through streets framed by piles of rubble, ruined steel mills, partly rebuilt workers' housing teeming with gaunt children and gray-faced adults, on her way from school toward her Aunt Gertrud's flat. She has been with Aunt Gertrud and Uncle Heinz since her mother was taken to hospital. Weeks have felt like years: cold, gray, interminable. She climbs dark stairs, rings the doorbell, sheds shoes and satchel in a place that doesn't smell like home.

The oranges are mounded on Aunt Gertrud's kitchen counter. Anna longs to touch them, press waxy skins against her cheek, inhale their unfamiliar scent. She has never seen a citrus fruit.

"Hands off," Aunt Gertrud snaps.

Uncle Heinz proffers a single orange section to Anna that first night, after he demonstrates and details how to peel: Slice the rind in an exact circle around the tiny scar that marks the top. Then, slide the penknife downward, away from the circumcision, like tracing lines of longitude, each line precise, not too deep, just enough to nick the skin. Then ease each piece of rind away from the fruit, deliberately, evenly, one by one.

Each morning after this first night, the pile of glowing orbs will be smaller than the night before, a sunset that lasts for days or weeks. Gertrud and Heinz eat in secret, after they send Anna off to bed. Each night, her mind will replay her uncle's expounding voice. Each night she vows never to peel an orange in his way.

My mother's violent ritual, the rip-a-rip of rinds, the detonating limonene, have never changed over the fifty years I've watched. She cannot picture that her daughter, the botanist, now lives in a country so rich in oranges along the southern tips of both its coasts that peels from juice factories form mountains, enough to feed an industry with citrus oil, enough not just for perfumes and insecticides, but such excess that bottles of orange paint remover fill shelves of home improvement stores across a continent, enough to dissolve residues of centuries.

Stripped of its peel and white albedo, each orange turns into a globe inside my mother's hands. Translucent membranes barely contain pearls of juice. Botanically, an orange is a hesperidium, a modified golden berry whose name points to the evening star. Inside the tough rind, membranes between carpels inscribe meridians, as though it were a globe designed to share. My mother's thumb slides from pole to pole through Planet Orange's hollow core. Over and over, she divides the world, hands slices to my sister and to me until we raise our voices, begging her to stop. ◆

Betty Crocker's Unwritten Rules

LAYNIE TZENA

You may laugh, but Tenafly looked serious.

That's David, to you. People from New Jersey (don't call it Joisey, and please stop saying "What exit?") often call each other by the name of their home town. I understand that one of my temple friends is Myrna to some people, but her real name is Springfield.

Call me Plainfield.

Anyway: Way back when my sister was still speaking to the rest of the family, we were in the kitchen after a recipe had proven false. Now, you can trust my recipes. I have eaten all of them, and here I am still writing to you.

But this recipe was apparently tested on the author's children, who, it is said, immediately ran away from home, and possibly on some species that promptly became extinct. It was called "Wonderful Old-Fashioned Gingerbread." It was not wonderful. It did not taste like any other gingerbread I have ever had, before or since—possibly because of the yogurt. Maybe it was old-fashioned. It was not allowed to grow old.

Well, wait a minute. The "fashion" in "old-fashioned"—that's not a lie. The recipe actually came from a then-popular cookbook. So it was fashionable. Just not edible.

So I thought, let's just crumble it and add some other things to it and make cookies. At which point my sister, who had only moments ago been reminding me that I must always sit in the middle when we rode in the car with Mommy because if I sat on the end I would fall out, invoked Betty Crocker's Unwritten Rule #1: "Thou shalt not make cookies from baked cake."

I obeyed. (You try arguing with her. Besides, she might have been right. But that's classified.)

But when I told Tenafly about Joyce Goldstein's Salmon with Pistachio Sauce, and he said he didn't like salmon, and I said, "So substitute chicken," he tried to invoke Betty Crocker's Unwritten Rule #2 (though he didn't call it that; that was my sister's idea), and proclaimed, "You can't substitute chicken for fish." And the very French friend of an American friend, after a dinner party for which a chicken had given its life, provided Betty Crocker's Unwritten Rule #3, letting pass that she "would never serve chicken to my guests." (Rumor has it she somehow managed to eat a fair amount of it, though.)

Fortunately, I have just located my magic wand. I am now waving it, and pronouncing some words in a language very few people speak. But I am a trained professional. And, as they say in a language many people do speak: No charge.

And what do you know? You are now free to substitute chicken for fish, fish for chicken (though you probably won't catch any), serve chicken to your guests, and whatever else comes to mind.

And since we're mostly grown now, I hope it's OK to say that Betty Crocker, lovely as she might have been in that Ozzie-and-Harriet kind of way, never existed. ◆

Finding Home

CHARLOTTE WHITTY

"When you're homesick," I advised my children when they struck out into the world, "chop an onion. It'll help, I promise."

It's what I do; it works every time.

It's not complicated. You don't need a plan. But if you're homesick, or you have the blues, all you need to do is remember to *chop an onion*. Before you know it, the bacon fat is melted in the cast iron, you're tipping that onion in, and it starts to speak to you in your mother tongue. It whispers sweet nothings in your ear as it sizzles in the pan and fills the air with its delectable aroma.

Then, you're mincing garlic, examining the contents of the veggie drawers in your fridge, and contemplating the plastic containers and baggies in your freezer. You find yourself swaying your hips side to side and singing soulfully along with Irma Thomas about a hard rain that brings back memories, even though you can't carry a tune. Snippets of olfactory recollections slip into your head like snapshots, as the bell pepper and celery become tender in your sauté—hallelujah! The Holy Trinity is present.

All of a sudden you're thirteen years old, walking into the kitchen after school on an early spring afternoon. The doorframe next to the yellow phone, which matches the flowers on the wall where it hangs, is packed up and down with phone numbers, messages, and notes, scribbled in various colors at random angles, like a road map of Paris. You pass the open window where the breakfast table is and catch a glimpse of the fruit bowl, currently populated with bananas and apples, each bearing a different expression, idly inked by your mother during a conversation. You feel the gentle breeze, with leftover cool around its edges from the subtropical winter. You get a whiff of the perfect, orange-blossom fragrance of pittosporum as it wafts in to mingle with your mother's cooking. There she is, standing over the hot stove dressed in brown, double-knit slacks with nothing on top but a brassiere, stirring her roux.

Now Dr. John is crooning in a gravelly voice, with his New Orleans accent, about goin' back home to fill up on étouffée, as you add the okra, harvested and frozen in the late summer for such a winter's feast. You pour in a can of crushed roasted tomatoes that had been gathering dust in the pantry, toss in a bay leaf and the minced garlic, add some salt and pepper, a little Tabasco, set the top on the pan, and lower the heat to simmer.

The house is filled with the smell of home. As the rice cooks, you dance to the music of Professor Longhair. He's in your kitchen, ticklin' the ivories to the tune of "Tipitina." That's the name of the bar where you made out with a stranger while the Wild Tchoupitoulas, decked out in pounds of shimmering, brightly colored feathers, sang about the Mardi Gras Indians, one Fat Tuesday eve long ago.

You glance out your kitchen window, just above the sink. You see fat, furry snowflakes falling fast and thick and realize you are somewhere else, but you've made it home, if only for a moment. ◆

I Cooked This for You

MARK GREENSIDE

My friend, neighbor, and guardian angel, Madame P, has invited me to dinner with her, Monsieur, and her grandson, Daniel. We've had aperitifs and nibbles and are sitting at the table, in the center of which is a huge covered bowl. The settings are simple: a plate, a glass for water, a glass for wine, a tablespoon, dinner knife and fork, and tiny picking implements that look to me like dental equipment. Madame uncovers the bowl, and Daniel goes over the top when he sees what's inside. I do, too, as I look at dozens of the ugliest shrimp I've ever seen piled on top of each other like a holocaust. What I see next is worse.

Madame digs into the bowl with her bare hand, grabs a handful of these orangey-pink things, and drops them in a mound onto my plate, saying, "Langoustines."

I look at the pile in front of me: bulging bodies, appendages akimbo, whiskers, feelers, tiny iridescent orange eggs, and big, shiny, beady black eyes staring up at me. I sit there with my hands in my lap, staring back.

The good news is they're not moving. The better news is neither am I. No way am I touching them, let alone eating them. Then, I watch horrified as Daniel breaks the head off one of them and sucks on the thorax with delight. He lifts one of the picks and scrapes the insides out like a dentist cleaning plaque. Everyone is happy—except me.

I know it's rude not to eat these things, or at least taste them, especially since Madame cooked this treat, this specialty straight from the Atlantic, still breathing and crawling when she got out of bed early this morning to buy them, for me. I also know it's not polite to throw up on the table, and that's what will happen if I put one near my mouth.

Monsieur passes me the bread. I cut a piece and butter it, pretty sure there's no going wrong with that. Crispy baguette and rich, creamy butter—forget Campbell's soup: *this* is mmmm, mmmm, good.

I chew my bread and watch Madame, Monsieur, and Daniel demolish the mounds in front of them and reach into the bowl for more. Piles of black, beady-eyed heads, pieces of pink exoskeleton and carapace, shell splinters, whiskers, feelers, and glowing teensy orange eggs litter their plates and the table all around them, making a mess. The space in front of me is spotless. Until this moment, I thought cleanliness was godliness to Madame. Now I see there's a higher order, and gustatory pleasure and need trumps all: clean plate tops clean house. Meanwhile, Monsieur keeps filling the wine glasses, and I keep emptying mine.

Finally, Madame reaches across the table and removes my plate. Thank God, I think, as I watch her snap the heads off a dozen more of the guys and gals, crack their torsos between her thumb and forefinger, and peel away the shells and carapaces to expose the corpses. I'm elated—until she puts the plate back in front of me with a look that says, "I cooked this for *you*!"

Daniel and Monsieur stop eating and watch.

On my plate are small chunks of white meat looking like brain or tumors or worse. I fork the smallest piece possible and drown it in Madame's homemade mayonnaise, bite, chew, and swallow. The mayonnaise is great. I fork another piece and dip it in the mayonnaise. It tastes like lobster, crab, and shrimp combined. I fork another and another and another and clean my plate.

The langoustines are followed by lotte, a dense, chunky, white fish, like halibut. I clean my plate again. It's lucky for us I've never seen a lotte or heard of it, because when I do, I see it's one of the ugliest fish in the world— all head, no body, which means what I ate were cheeks. Fish cheeks! Holy Christ! What's next? All I know for certain is there will be a next, and whatever it is, and whenever it comes, I won't be ready. *Jamais prêt, toujours surpris.* Such is my life in France: never ready, always surprised. ◆

Learning

SHERRIE FLICK

There I am. I'm little with little hands, watching you cut rhubarb from our back yard into tiny chunks. You give me a piece and then laugh when I pucker. I'm little, and it's summer. I'm on a chair and there's sunlight in our kitchen, birds outside, gravel in our driveway.

The big pine tree is still standing, and so are the apple trees. You are making pie and this moment is an important one in my life, but who would guess it? I'm watching your big hands roll pie crust—the sleek wooden rolling pin, the little white measuring cup of extra flour beside the white glass canisters: sugar, flour, tea bags. An open bag of flour sits ready to fill in, if necessary.

The rolling pin has a cotton tube around it. It smells homey and moist. Everything seems good and mysterious and breezy, and you are rolling the piecrust, and it is magic to me.

The lump of tan dough spreads itself into one circle, then another. The first goes into the bottom of the pie pan. The second stays on the counter in a drizzle of flour. I'm watching, and I'm paying attention in a way I will only realize years later when I roll my crust smoothly, when I slice my apples thinly into a bowl, when I pull my own pie from my own oven and put it on my cooling rack and know it's beautiful. And I won't know exactly why pie means home to me no matter where I'm living. But it will. It does.

And now I watch you cut and slash little marks here and there. I watch you fill and fold and form the iconic zigzag of the crust. It's beautiful, I think, then—it's a mystery, this putting together, this one complete thing.

I am little and I don't even like pie yet. I don't like pie for years to come. But now look—there is my little pie pan beside yours, my little rolling pin with red handles. There I am, and I'm learning. ◆

Breakfast Served Daily

MAUREEN MANCINI AMATURO

There's nothing easy about eggs over easy. Usually, I miss the pan. Often, I flip only half, and always, I leave some of it drooling onto something it shouldn't. And I hate frying bacon because then the house smells all day. So, I don't do it. Pancakes throw my schedule off. My family will eat cereal, but only as a snack at the most unexpected times. They always ask me to buy cream cheese, but I think it's just to see how long they have to wait to see the mold grow. And my kids will never forgive Kellogg's for frozen waffles. Not the biggest issue in my life. Strangely, breakfast doesn't have rules in my house, though eating and cooking for my family is my core focus, as it was for the all the mothers on my family tree. Breakfast just isn't popular. Let's be honest. It's not the most social meal, in America anyway. But sometimes I think if American breakfasts were more like those in Europe—except Germany, where they serve salami and blood sausage at 7 a.m.—I could make breakfast a thing again. Like in Paris: a croissant, a crusty roll, orange marmalade, and hot chocolate daily. Yes and yum, and that's why sixty million French people can't be wrong.

Come to think of it, I don't even remember eating breakfast in Italy. Was probably still full from those nine-course, 10 p.m. dinners. Forget England. Nothing was edible in England. Or Scotland. I tried a Scotch egg. What a surprise, and not in a good way. Could this be where Dr. Seuss discovered green eggs and ham? I couldn't eat breakfast in Wales. Too early in the morning to deal with a menu that doesn't use vowels.

Never once did I yearn for an American breakfast in Belgium. That was all chocolate all the time. Sometimes on a waffle, but not necessarily in the morning. I'm giving Madrid a half star—chorizo and a cup of chocolate to dip it in. Guess which part gets the star. Denmark was wedges of cheese and a side of jelly. In Austria, someone said the food on the dish was rabbit. No thank you. I don't know what was on the breakfast table in Sweden. I couldn't look. Liechtenstein, lovely, little Liechtenstein. They don't eat breakfast. It's a small country. Amsterdam. I remember two things about Amsterdam. We were not allowed to eat french fries on the canal boats, and there was a marijuana store on every corner. I think people eat breakfast all day there. I remember something else. There was a local pub named Café Hell, but I don't think they served breakfast. Portugal was a problem. Seafaring people that they are, they built every meal around fish. I hate seafood, and everything was cooked in 10W-40. Luckily, I had my gall bladder removed before that trip.

But none of that is my daily reality. I live with the American breakfast, whatever that is. Last I heard, it's anything with at least fifteen grams of protein and a carton of coconut water, but maybe that trend ended earlier today. Hold on, it just switched to avocado toast. Stay tuned. American food trends change every hour on the half hour. Definitely not as reliable as Paris's morning bread and marmalade. Anyway, I hold this truth to be self-evident: Like most things in America, breakfast can be whatever I make of it. So, the American breakfast is not as romantic or exotic as some of the vacation breakfasts I've faced. At home, I may wake up to a tub of moldy cream cheese (wait, does mold count as a houseplant?), but I'm still grateful I don't live in Portugal waking up to oily fish. ◆

Dinner at Five

ELAINE CRAUDER

I set the table every evening at five o'clock. Knife and spoon go on the right of the plate. Fork rests on top of the folded cloth napkin on the left.

Dad drops off his briefcase by his home office in the den. He peers out and asks, "So, what's for dinner?" I laugh, and shrug. He laughs back, and says, "You never know." Mom prepares meat loaf, creamed chipped beef, and casseroles upon casseroles.

Mornings, my family is a whirlwind of collecting notebooks and binders, getting out in a rush after a cold breakfast. Dinner, however, is an every-night family gathering, promptly at 5:30—it is the Midwest and the 1970s.

Mom starts teaching at the university when I am in middle school and assigns Monday to Thursday dinners to my older brother and me. She knows it is impossible to do it all.

Monday's meal (my turn) is a pound of ground beef sautéed until browned and the juicy fat bubbles. I stir in a can of condensed cream of mushroom soup, along with a pound of cooked elbow noodles. Topping off the meal is a package of frozen peas, which I proudly boil until the rounds are wrinkled— the way Dad likes them. Mom thinks they are mushy.

Tuesday's dinner (my brother's turn) is a pound of ground beef sautéed until browned and the juicy fat bubbles. He adds a can of condensed tomato soup, along with a pound of cooked elbow noodles. Topping off the meal is a package of frozen corn and peas, which he boils until very hot—the way Mom likes them. Dad thinks they aren't done.

Wednesday's dinner (me)—repeat from Monday.

Thursday's dinner (my brother)—repeat from Tuesday.

I am giddy with anticipation all day on Friday, for Mom brings home Arby's roast beef sandwiches with special sauce. Topping off the meal is whole fruit: bananas, apples, or for a treat, pears.

By ninth grade, I specialize in an amazing company dish: spaghetti with meat sauce. The secret begins with a generously poured glug of olive oil;

add chopped—not pressed—garlic, bay leaf, and oregano. Barely brown the garlic before dropping in the bay leaf and oregano. It goes without saying the dish needs canned, diced tomato and plenty of leftover Chianti.

Bubble gently for an hour and stir when you feel like it. Top with freshly grated Parmesan. Serve over spaghetti with a side of cooked but not overdone peas.

Dessert for guests is Mom's specialty, pineapple upside-down cake. It is a miracle every time the pan is tipped over and pineapple slices appear *on top*, with a maraschino cherry in the middle of each ring. The house smells delicious and the only thing better than the moist cake is the Reddi Wip bought for the occasion.

All through high school I am amazed how well pineapple upside-down cake goes with spaghetti and sauce. Mom and I are a team, though we don't use those words; we just work together in the kitchen, catching up on our days.

I've lived on the East Coast for years. The stores—like they do throughout the country—stock multiple shelves of canned soups. Condensed and otherwise. I almost never buy them.

Decades after leaving home, I make pasta for dinner with a vegetarian red sauce and a heaping salad. In midwinter, simply baked sweet potatoes and sheet-pan broccoli roasted in the oven with extra virgin olive oil, salt, and pepper. My plates are red with sauce on yellow-tinged pasta; green with salad; or orange with sweet potatoes and green with broccoli. Nothing condensed. Dinner has mushroomed.

Occasionally, on a bone-chilling winter afternoon, I'll call Mom early, before the sun sets at five. Not like my usual after-*Jeopardy* call, daily since Dad died a few years ago. Mom and I know that the best comfort food is grilled cheese (cheddar, please) buttered on both sides. With warmed soup: preferably creamed, condensed, tomato.

When I call, Mom says, "Let me turn down the stove." I wait. She picks up the receiver. "OK, I'm ready." I can almost hear her take a spoonful of soup, then a bite of grilled cheese. "Nothing like it," she says.

I sip my tea; five is too early for my dinner. As though we're sitting at the same kitchen table, across from each other rather than a few hundred miles apart, Mom and I begin to catch up on our day. ◆

Foie Gras or Faux Pas?

TOM HAZUKA

Growing up, I never ate anything even remotely adventurous. The closest thing was probably the one time my mother served liver, though the word "ate" is debatable because I'm not sure I managed to swallow a single revolting bite. Before you dismiss me as a pathetic wuss, let me preemptively mention that I've eaten beef tongue in Chile and cicadas in China, and quite enjoyed both. In China I also learned that fish must always be presented whole; it would be an insult to serve what I would prefer: a lovely fillet that spares me the hassle of dealing with bones.

This set me to pondering how easy it can be to commit food faux pas, the gastronomic equivalent of the crowd at the Concert for Bangladesh applauding Ravi Shankar, only to be told that Ravi was glad they enjoyed the tuning, and he hoped they would like the actual music as well. I'm not talking about unadventurous eaters who go to McDonald's in Paris and turn up their noses at anything unfamiliar. I'm talking about folks with open minds about food and other cultures who sometimes make false steps because, after all, this is an imperfect world.

Recently arrived in Fribourg, Switzerland, for our junior year abroad, some friends and I went out to dinner. Jim Kane ordered steak tartare. We were all curious to see this undoubtedly delicious Swiss way of preparing steak. When the waiter served Jim a plate displaying a mound of raw hamburger, we were creeped out by the restaurant's mistake but played it cool, politely reminding the waiter that Jim had ordered steak. The unsmiling *serveur* explained the uncooked truth about steak tartare, and thus did four young Americans have their culinary horizons expanded—sort of. None of us dared to actually taste this new horizon, and Jim ordered a regular steak and *pommes frites* to replace it.

My next food misadventure came a few weeks later, while I was staying with a family in Clermont-Ferrand, France. French meals are served one course at a time, and at one meal Madame Bessat placed in front of me a plate laden with strips of fresh-cut carrots. I despaired. Cooked carrots I can handle, but raw carrots make me gag. Yes, I know they're healthy food, and I wish I liked them, but I just don't. I fought gamely, downing prodigious quantities of bread in a vain attempt to mask the taste of each gnarly bite, but I had hardly made a dent in the pile before Mom, Dad and the two sons had finished and were trying to pretend not to stare at me. Finally, figuring that words were less impolite than bolting to the bathroom to barf, I confessed. Of course they understood, and told me to just speak up if it happened again. (It didn't.) They already thought I was a bizarre eater because I had requested milk with meals (I can't begin to understand that today. Really, Tom? Milk?) The oddness went both ways, though, when I discovered that their milk came in liter cartons, unrefrigerated until opened.

After college I joined the Peace Corps. My first week in Santiago, Chile, I went to a cafe for lunch. Knowing little Spanish yet, I played it safe and ordered from among the few menu items I recognized: *una hamburguesa y una cerveza.* When a sweating bottle of Cristal pilsener and a hamburger arrived, I squirted on ketchup from the plastic bottle and took a bite. I knew the stereotype about fiery Latin cuisine, but was still surprised at how *picante* that mouthful was. My sips of beer turned to gulps to try and quench the fire. I ordered another beer and slathered on more ketchup to mask the heat, but every bite seemed hotter than the last. I feared looking like an ugly American if I left the burger half-eaten, as if the food weren't good enough for me. Not to mention the shame of being so un-macho that I couldn't even handle a hamburger. I ordered a third Cristal, squeezed on lots more ketchup, and forced myself to finish, then walked out into the sunshine unexpectedly tipsy and with a singed mouth, wondering how I could possibly survive this food for two years.

My new Chilean friends burst out laughing when they heard the story. The hamburger wasn't the problem, Gringo, they told me. That red stuff you poured on to fix the problem wasn't ketchup, it was *ají*—hot pepper sauce! ◆

Friday Service

ALLEGRA GRANT

Each Friday I perform an act of service early in the morning, just as the sun peeks over the mountains when I walk into the kitchen. Within the past six months, the chef I work for decided to develop a beef butchery program for the restaurant. She made a decision to purchase a forequarter of beef to utilize between her two restaurants.

Throughout the seasonal changes I have seen the beef program grow into something beautiful. My chef hired highly trained, professional butchers to instruct our management team of chefs how to butcher the forequarter. With their guided instruction, we have developed the butchery program very quickly and have been utilizing as much of the forequarter as we can. The beef is dry aged and we do lose some meat that is near the mold, but we do our very best to utilize all that we can between the bones and beneath the fat.

The service I perform and attend each Friday is honest nourishment for my mind, body, and soul as a human being.

For nearly two hours, I spend my morning in reflection with this forequarter of the carcass, anchoring my knife against the rib bones and separating the meat to reserve for further creations. These two hours are sacred each and every time, because I separate myself from the hustle and bustle of the start of a busy prep day to pay homage to this animal.

You might think, "Wow, two hours is a lot of time devoted to cleaning the bones and fat of a cow," but in actuality that is not even a fraction of the time that is invested in raising, slaughtering and butchering ethical meat.

Today, as I was cleaning the bones, I thought about where this beautiful beast lived out its last days. Whenever I close my eyes for a brief moment to breathe in the aroma of the aged beef, I can almost smell the grass where this animal lay. It is a perfect image in my mind each Friday morning. To me, it's curious that I spend my Fridays in this manner, because Jesus sacrificed his body on a Friday.

As a Catholic, I abstain from eating meat during Lent on Fridays, which helps me to practice self-awareness and patience and to attain greater communion with Christ. It is not required of me to clean the bones as heavily as I choose, but it is what I believe to be honest with myself as a servant of God to do this work.

This is my Friday service. ◆

Tortillas

LEEANNA TORRES

Jessica writes about tortillas.

My cousin writes like she knows what she's talking about, writes loosely and wildly, and a resentment grows within me, deep and wide, suddenly and surprisingly. My resentment takes a sharp shape, jagged and blue.

"Tortillas are a staple in our home," begins Jessica's blog, and I can feel the exclamation point at the end of her statement even though it is not there. I read the words of her blog not because I have to, but because something drives me there, again and again, to read what she's going to write about *this* time, her private life scattered out on a website for all the world to see.

Jessica writes about tortillas.

"I remember standing on my tippy-toes on a stool in Tomé, New Mexico, watching my Nana make homemade flour tortillas. I was amazed this small but mighty woman could knead and roll out dough with such intensity. I also distinctly remember that there was no recipe in sight ..."

Reading Jessica's blog makes me wonder not at the notion of memory, but rather of the things we choose to write about, the items we pick out of memory and keep as our own. Why has Jessica taken the small, soft, sacred family legacy of making tortillas and put it onto a page with such casualness?

Jessica writes about tortillas, but she leaves out the description of the kitchen, the smell in the air, the look of flour on my Nana's hands, some of it caught up beneath her silver wedding ring, the ring she never took off, not even as a widow. She leaves out mention of the *bolillo*, the small wood and handle-less rolling pin. She leaves out the sad look my Nana often hid even in her quietness, her hands working in flour, her voice as soft as the fading color of white along the walls of her small kitchen.

Instead Jessica writes and types and posts, and her writing and blogging seems so loose to me, so quickly put together, with so little room for detail or refinement. But what is it that makes me angry about Jessica's blog?

"*Writing about life, love, and everything in-between*," boasts the blog. I wince at the soft colors she's chosen for her page—cotton-candy pink, baby blue, a collage of polka dots and up-close photos of her favorite foods.

I'm pissed because *I* don't have a blog. I'm angry at Jessica's blog because she can be honest and revealing and open and available, and I cannot. Instead, I sit alone and complain to my computer screen, wondering if there is enough vodka in the house to get me drunk.

Jessica's blog is catchy, entertaining, fun.

Our Nana made tortillas. She signed her name using her left hand, but rolled tortillas with both hands, all in. The *manteca* (lard) used for the tortillas was from our annual family *matanza*, when an entire pig was slaughtered and the meat and lard stored for the rest of the year. Nana's *manteca* was never store-bought. And from what I remember, Nana never removed her rings when she worked in the kitchen, but let the ingredients—flour, water, salt—work their way into the places and spaces of silver and diamond as carelessly as a sigh.

The world of writing is changing, from paper to blog, from printed to "posted." Even now I type more often rather than physically write. Everything changes, always. I sit at my desk milling through a "draft" manuscript that may never be seen, while Jessica rushes into her blog with urgency and excitement to be seen by all. Who is the *real* writer? Whose work is worth being "published"?

Nana used to make tortillas, placing each one on the *comal* (griddle) to cook with a discipline that to this day is unattainable for me. With the calmest confidence, Nana was often quiet during family conversations, listening more than talking, smiling softly more than laughing loudly. Nana still remains a kind of mystery to me, a woman who taught us through action and example rather than rantings or words. And now Jessica and I are both writers, memories of food and *familia* filtering through us both.

We are writing in a world of change, always changing. Jessica writes about tortillas and all I do is eat them. And perhaps Nana is somewhere smiling at us both, neither of us right or wrong, paper or blog, writing to right our own memories and wants, Nana never loving us any less for what we do or do not say. ◆

All Ten Provinces and Both Territories

H. E. CASSON

My grandmother gave me a coin collection, one quarter for each province and territory inset in a brightly colored map of Canada. The cardboard holder was slid into a plastic sleeve, which said *this gift is valuable.* The coins were shiny, uncirculated; a sheath of not-really silver, given to each of the twelve grandchildren, purchased at the post office in the mall.

When I was kicked out, I left with two black garbage bags of things. Things meant clothes. Things meant books. Things meant my Cabbage Patch Kid. Things meant a plastic sleeve with one quarter for every province and territory.

Here is what it feels like to leave a place that is supposed to be home with only two black garbage bags of things: decimation. To decimate something is to destroy 10 percent. I am sure I lost at least 10 percent of myself, like popping out a coin and seeing that, really, it is just a hole in printed cardboard, and the quarter, no matter how pretty, is just a quarter. Goodbye Saskatchewan.

There was almost a year between leaving with two black garbage bags of things and sitting, legs crossed, in a rented room in the house of a Seventh Day Adventist. She turned off my heat to save money and sang hymns at night to save my soul. Neither worked. She sold the house, and my soul? At least another 10 percent froze off under every piece of clothing I owned, praying to any god who would listen, even hers. Goodbye Newfoundland.

Here is what an empty belly feels like: feral. If you've ever heard a story about a person who resorted to theft or prostitution or murder or cannibalism because they were starving and thought, "I could never ..." you should know that you are wrong. You would. To be that hungry is to be feral.

Hunger leaks from the body like sweat. Like tears. Chewing the insides of my cheeks, drinking water to feel full, I had cracked every unlabeled can bought for a dime. I had finished other people's lunches. I had asked for quarters to make an important call and used them to buy cookies at the cafeteria. Four quarters bought three still-hot cookies, the chocolate and sweet melting over every taste bud.

I was feral and I sat crossed-legged on the floor of my rented room in the home of a Seventh Day Adventist and pulled the printed piece of cardboard out of the plastic sheath. I popped out all ten provinces and both territories. Pop, pop, pop.

I did not think about putting them back in, rebuilding Alberta and Ontario. I counted them to make sure I had enough.

I held them in my hand. I didn't put them in my pocket or a wallet. I needed to feel them. Nova Scotia. Prince Edward Island. Quebec. I held them so tight they didn't jingle. I pressed their pictures into my skin.

I walked out of my room, out of the house, out onto the street. I turned left. The sidewalk felt solid and I was grateful. I went to the pizza shop and stood in line behind moms, with babes in arms, picking up an easy dinner, and men fresh off work grabbing a slice on the way home.

Two slices and a pop cost $3, tax in.

"Oh! You got the pretty ones!" He counted out the coins.

"Thanks." I took the two slices, one folded over the other, on a white paper plate. Grease was already soaking it, making the plate stained glass, with light shining through. Holy, holy, holy. I sat on the curb and took one bite, the small triangle bite that's mostly cheese, right at the tip. The perfect bite. I held it in my mouth. I let the oil fill my throat. I bent the cheese around my tongue. I chewed slowly. The longer you chew, the better food tastes. I fought the urge to eat it quickly, fill myself up. Goodbye Manitoba.

I ate it as deliberately as I could, filling in holes and patching cracks. I went back to my room and threw the stained-glass plate and the empty cardboard Canada in a black plastic garbage bag and climbed under every piece of clothing I owned to go to sleep, for once, full. ◆

Buffalo Gourmet

ERIC D. LEHMAN

Someone asked me recently what my favorite gourmet food was, and I answered buffalo wings. It was not the answer she expected, and she laughed, thinking I was joking. I was not. After all, a gourmet food is one that takes a lot of care and time to prepare, one that expends a lot of culinary effort. Buffalo wings fit this definition perfectly. They are a response to an age-old problem: what to do with the thin end of a chicken's long arm? Well, drown it in spicy sauce, dip it in blue cheese, and make it a meal. Sometimes this tiny piece of mostly grease and fat is even fried or baked a second time. That's a lot of work for very little payoff. Why go to all this trouble?

Because they are delicious, that's why. Chewing the hot flesh off the tiny bones, nibbling the last gobbets of tissue, has become a national pastime. And though part of our love is licking sauce-stained fingers, somehow eating "buffaloed" cauliflower or calamari isn't quite the same.

I experienced my first great buffalo wings during my first year of college at the University of Delaware. I spent most of that year alone, walking the cracked sidewalks of Newark, and early on found CR Wings in the shopping center, where I began my descent into addiction and shame. This was before the foodie revolution, and a restaurant only selling buffalo wings was unusual. What was even more unusual was the incredible quality of their secret sauce. No matter how spicy they made them, the wings still tasted wonderful, and I went back week after week. These became my standard for the rest of my life, as I made pilgrimages to the best wings restaurants in America.

Today, wings come in many flavors, and each restaurant has its own specialty, from lemon pepper to Jamaican saltfish, from kung pao to Coca-Cola. But the Anchor Bar's original combination of red-hot sauce, butter, and vinegar seems to have outlasted them all. How to describe that magical taste? Savory, tangy, and spicy, but not too much—there must be a balance between heat and flavor. Rookie wing makers just dump on chili pepper, thinking hotter is better, or perhaps compensating for poor quality meat. Usually if a wing is too spicy, the taste leaves, or it ends up just tasting like a chili pepper. Once in a while, a great wing chef will find a secret mixture that will meld fine flavor with stomach-searing intensity. But more often, the best wings have a fine heat without being "nuclear" or "suicide" level. Those are for television challenges and not for enjoyment.

The trick is making the sauce thick enough so that when applied to the wings, it doesn't burn off. Layering is the key, with multiple brushings between raw and cooked. The wings should be large enough so you are not just eating skin, but get them too large and you'll defeat the purpose. After all, this is not an exercise in protein-packing, it is a gourmet experience. Breading or battering is another example of an attempt to cover up shortcomings, or a misapplication of chicken frying technique. And as far as dipping in blue cheese or ranch dressing, first establish whether the wing's taste is strong enough so the salad dressing won't drown the flavor.

It is not often that a perfect solution is found for a food problem. From now until civilization collapses, some version of these buffalo wings will probably exist, and the rest is just fiddling with fractions. They are gourmet fare in the best sense of the word, a hoof-to-tail delicacy, a formerly useless piece of foodstuff turned into a chef's necessity. They may not be expensive or considered haute cuisine, but they are debated over, argued over, even fought over. When did anyone fight so hard over caviar? When did oyster-stuffed lobsters with a truffle cream sauce inspire such devotion? I'll keep searching for the finest hot wings until my stomach lining disappears, and I am not alone. ◈

Comfort Food

LISA OHLEN HARRIS

I woo Jeanne's appetite with her favorite Southern foods. Grits, banana pudding, Miracle Whip, and bologna loaf on white bread. French dressing over cottage cheese. Sausage gravy over biscuits: pallid sauce so thick with grease that the leftovers will congeal, gray and lumpy. Tomorrow I will reheat them to mash over her toast.

When she first moved in with us I made things my way: stir fry, one-pot dishes, beans and rice. She ate only after fishing out the veggies. If I used tofu, she asked, "What's this stuff?" and pushed it aside. And yet she bragged, "Lisa is such a good cook!" Years passed and I learned to reserve a handful of raw veggies for her plate; she loved vegetables, as it ended up—just not cooked.

Back when I was Todd's girlfriend, Jeanne invited her minister and his wife, among others, to a dinner party. She cut the greens quickly with scissors and tossed the salad in a large trash bag. She made the entire meal a day ahead, so when the guests arrived we all were relaxed and ready, and all she had to do was reheat. I remember chicken Parmesan that night, a salad with honeyed almonds and red onions. I remember the smell of garlic cheese bread rising as my future mother-in-law's minister said grace. I remember bringing the savory bread to my mouth and crunching in to find that, instead of garlic butter, under the melted cheese she had spread Miracle Whip, warm and cloying. After a long wash of ice water to get the hunk down, I poked at the rest of my meal.

Once I had a ring on my finger, I volunteered to make the cheese bread whenever she cooked Italian. And when I had the Harris name firmly attached to my own by vows, I also picked the red onions out of my salad and laid them on the side of my plate.

In recipes calling for milk I now substitute heavy cream. Jeanne has lost seven pounds in two weeks and we're not sure why, except the doctor says the mass in her lungs—three months ago the size of the doctor's retractable pen clicker—is now the size of both his hands fisted one over the other.

What the tests will show, what the future will be, I do not know. What I do know is this: break the sausage apart as it fries in the pan; sprinkle in flour to absorb the grease; add heavy cream and stir until the sauce is thick and no lumps remain. Spoon the mixture over biscuits or toast and grind fresh pepper on top. When I bring it to her, the plate will be warm through. She will take it and eat. ◆

Arrival

SARI FORDHAM

We travel to Finland through our kitchen cupboard. On hot California days or on long days or on days when she just wants lingonberries, my five-year-old daughter Kai crams herself into the empty knife cupboard and shouts, "I'm going to Finland."

"Me, too," I say, crowding my legs in behind her. The magic happens and Kai is eating lingonberries straight off a bush, while I stuff *piirakka* into my mouth. And then we continue on with our lives.

I don't remember when we started our silliness. Probably sometime after Kai first visited Finland. She was a toddler then, making this our longest-running game. But for me, it goes back much further. I have always traveled to Finland through the kitchen.

My mother came to America in 1963 to get her master's degree in English. Her tuition was paid for by the Finnish government with the expectation that she would return and teach. Instead, she married my father, had two daughters, and decided that we would be Americans.

She spoke only English to Sonja and me, drawing a linguistic border between us and her. When we visited Finland, our American mouths made flat American sounds, and our American ears gathered little from the lilting syllables around us. Our taste buds, however, assured us that in at least one important way, we belonged.

Sonja and I ate lingonberries with new potatoes. We ate rye bread and cheese. With our cousins, we foraged for currants and then snatched apples off the table and carried them into the forest. In the evening, Sonja and I choked down glasses of buttermilk, and we made faces over the cabbage rolls our aunt diligently made. There was also salted licorice, the world's most perfect confection. And, of course, with every meal we ate *piirakka*.

When friends ask, I have a hard time describing it.

"It's like a hand pie, with a rye crust, and it's usually filled with a savory rice porridge."

"Here, let me show you." I type *piirakka* into the computer, trying to remember how many i's, how many k's, finally pulling up an image. The *piirakka* pictured are more beautiful than anything I produce. The edges are evenly crimped and the rice is golden brown.

A memory: My mother is in the kitchen, unusually flustered. "Look at them. They're like ugly cows." She is rolling out dough, spreading rice across it, pinching, scowling. She shoos me away.

When I was 25, my mother died. I was old enough to take care of myself, young enough that I hadn't learned her recipes. We had cooked in parallel. She made Finnish food; I cooked American food beside her. Part of it was my fault: I hated being told what to do. But when I once asked if I could help make *piirakka*, she said it was too much bother. Not the lesson, but the *piirakka* itself. "No one makes *piirakka* anymore." I now realize she doubted her abilities.

In her family, she was the unpractical daughter, hopeless in the kitchen. When she married my father, her signature dish was a fried egg served on lettuce. Slowly, she learned to make Finnish food, guided by memories. Around holidays we would eat *korvapuusti* and *piirakka*, her complaints about their appearance murmurs in the background. What I remember is that everything tasted so good. Like Finland.

After my mother died, I tried to recreate her recipes. She had left no written instructions, and so I searched online for help. I learned how to make an enriched pulla dough that I braided into loaves and fashioned into *korvapuusti*. Yet *piirakka* eluded me.

In Finland, almost no one makes them anymore. You buy them at the grocery store or from a home business. I'm a plane ticket away from all that easy *piirakka*, and so I try and try and try. Finally, I have it: a recipe that works. My *piirakka* look and taste like my mother's, which is to say I grumble about their appearance.

When Kai comes to help, I tell her they look like cows.

"Oh, Mommy," she says. "You are a silly mommy."

We work together, she at a small station beside me. I roll the dough thin, smooth on porridge with the back of a spoon, crimp the edges. I move the first batch to a cookie sheet and slide them into the oven.

We are traveling to Finland, and the timer is set for our arrival. ◆

Warsaw Market

CHRIS WIEWIORA

Brown water pooled on the uneven concrete pathway from the bus stop to the market. We didn't drive to the grocery store, because there wasn't one. I held onto Mom's hand. My red slicker airmailed by my Appalachian grandmother came to my knees. Rain slid down the material the same in Warsaw as in West Virginia.

Underneath the butcher's tin awning a man behind the counter practiced his English with Mom. She couldn't understand Polish, but she knew the sights and she talked to me as we shopped. The market had sections like a grocery store, but everything was outside. Mom told me that we weren't contained in one place to shop like we weren't contained by one language to speak.

At other stalls, Mom ordered in halting Polish. She tried to recall memorized phrases from Dad, who was Polish. I wondered if Dad was a language. If he was a language then was I half of that language? I was also half of Mom, but Mom had told me she could only speak Polish in the present tense. So, was I only Polish in Poland?

Mom spoke English and gestured for the butcher to lop off the feet and head of a chicken so it looked like one in the grocery stores back in the States. Mom told me she didn't mind paying a little more to make us feel more at home. I wondered where Mom thought was home for me: back in America as a Pole or in Poland as an American. I was too confused to ask what I would be in the future.

I knew I was in the present. I knew we were speaking two languages. I knew I didn't care how much anything cost, or even if Mom paid in złoties or dollars, as long as I got a pickle. I pointed for us to go to the next shopkeeper, the vegetable man. He didn't sell a glass jar that only grown-ups could twist and pop the seal and fork out a chip. He used a plastic bag as a glove and plunged his hand into the murky brine of a barrel. He handed me the plastic-wrapped pickle and I chomped on the crisp skin while Mom filled crosshatched nylon woven bags with mushrooms.

At a fruit pushcart, Mom selected what she said would always be quarts to her, not liters, of raspberries. For the thousandth time, Mom told me that she had craved them when she was pregnant with me. She had eaten them until she threw up. Mom's parents grew them in the hills of West Virginia and I had picked them outside. I knew how you just wanted to keep eating them, plucked under the sun that peeked out of the clouds above us.

Then, it seemed like the sun's rays spotlighted the baker's booth. Maybe it was just the smell of sourdough drifting to us. I pulled Mom to the shelves displaying rows of unsliced loaves. I had never seen whole bread with crusts browned almost black. My eyes glazed in front of the egg-washed pastries with dollops of cream at their centers. Mom told me that we would wait to buy bread back at the bakery in our neighborhood.

Grumpy, I imagined all the shopkeepers as trolls. Not evil, just bulbous. I knew their bodies were lumpy from toil like Americans behind counters. Nobody wore a uniform with a name tag or introduced themselves as Mister or Missus. Instead they might say, *Pan* or *Panni*. If not, then I only recognized if the Poles were men or women by the caps or shawls that covered their hair tucked behind their ears. I walked next to Mom, holding on with my non-pickle-smelly hand, and I watched the Poles' gaits—something between a waddle and a swagger—similar to Dad's mother. Since I was half would I walk one way or the other?

On our way out of the market, we stopped by the flower booth with bouquets in buckets. Mom's mother grew flowers and Dad's mother grew flowers. It didn't matter where we lived, there was beauty grown in the world. Mom picked a bunch of tulips and handed them to me. I held them upside-down. The yellow blossoms looked like empty cups that had held the rain and sun and air. ◆

Potatoes, Peas, and No, Please

ANUJA GHIMIRE

My father was living in a city six hours away for a job when I managed to make, more than once, decent fried potatoes with ginger, garlic, and onion. I had yet to understand that a side effect of a vivid imagination is extreme fear—the knife close to my thumb, ghee on the ladle catching fire, and oil splatters scattering temporary moles on my forearm. There was the gas stove holding explosions. Sitting on it like a mother hen, the pressure cooker and pending disasters.

But once a month, my father would come to town and ask that I make the tasty potatoes before he was on the road again. Even my mother had told her friends about the fried *aloo*. My sister, however, could cook pretty much anything by then. She had made spicy eggplant curry, rice, and *daal* for dinner when she was just eight. How she simply went to the kitchen and came out with meals was beyond me.

When my mother announced that a few of her work friends were going to visit the next day, I volunteered to make black-eyed peas, potatoes, and bamboo shoot curry and rice. It was my comprehensive final exam, and I knew what would be on the test. I had to trust myself.

I began with what I knew—soaking the legumes in a steel bowl filled with water and leaving it covered overnight. Step one was complete. Since cooking most curries follows the same basic recipe, I didn't ask my big sister or mother for help. After an uneventful day at school, in which I thought about everything that could go wrong with my *aloo bodi tama* curry, I braced myself for cooking. I immediately regretted declining my sister's offer to supervise or help. It was too late to be honest and wise now.

Presoaked rice was in the rice cooker after I had measured water volume with my index finger. I had minced ginger and garlic and chopped potatoes, tomatoes, chili peppers, and cilantro leaves. Overnight, the black-eyed peas had filled out into glistening, potent beans. I had already fried bamboo shoot pieces in vegetable oil and added turmeric. I began making the curry like I had learned by lots of watching and a little bit of cooking. Other than the pan nearly filling up with all the ingredients I put in, the cooking itself was uneventful.

My mother's friends could be heard in the living room downstairs. I had nothing to fear now. I thought about posing with a blushed face and hunched back to appear humble about my culinary skills. Should I thank all the aunties or just smile? I hadn't decided. Now, the last task was to offer a pinch on the stove as an offering to god and have a taste to formally revel in my glory. I brought a teaspoonful of *aloo bodi tama* curry to the tip of my tongue and immediately knew the biggest mistake I had made.

I could hear my mother saying, "Doesn't it smell so good? Now, even *sani* can cook." My sister was not on the balcony, so I couldn't confess to her or ask for help. After making sure the stove was turned off, I did what cowards do and ran down the stairs. I paused at the gate to make sure nobody was calling my name. I flung the gate open and, wiping my greasy hands on the sides of my frock, ran to my friend's house. She was in the middle of a tutoring session and gestured me to sit. I had run for twenty minutes to my friend's house, and I had to wait ten more minutes to tell her that I had put sugar instead of salt in the *aloo bodi tama* and that my mother and her friends had probably discovered the disaster by now. My friend laughed and offered me a samosa, which she hadn't made. The crisp, savory samosa stuffed with potatoes and peas only haunted me and formed a lump in my throat. The voice in my head saying "Come home now" was my mother's. ◆

True Grits

LYDIA OXENHAM

I had just moved to Knox County, Tennessee, when a recipe by the name of Easy Cheesy Shrimp & Grits caught my attention. Seeing as how my husband was returning home from the Carolinas, I planned to surprise him with dinner, it being a favorite meal of his and me being keen to please him after a long day's journey.

I traveled to Walmart in search of supplies, one of them being grits from Bob's Red Mill. They are yellow corn grits, known as polenta in other parts. I could not find them. I beseeched a store clerk to locate them for me. He directed me to the oatmeal section, in which I did find grits, but not from Bob's Red Mill. The small supply of grits was sheltered between oats that had been steel cut and oats that were rolled, all from the man known only as the Quaker.

I'd heard of the Quaker. He was a stern man, fond of cardiac well-being. But I had not known him to be so heartless until I returned home and inspected my wares. You see, the Quaker had sold me white corn grits, rather than the yellow corn my recipe called for. How foolish I was for trusting the Quaker rather than my own list of supplies! And when I acquainted myself with the Nutrition Facts Panel, I discovered these white corn grits were fortified with chemicals. I do not need a man in an oversize hat to fortify my food. Furthermore, these were quick-cooking grits, which is an insult to my judiciousness as a housewife.

The Quaker had no business selling grits in the first place, being known mainly for oats, that mighty versatile grain. Better he should leave grits to the experts at Bob's Red Mill.

Being short on time and long on embarrassment, I contemplated seeing my meal through with the Quaker's grits. But I've got too much pride to let my husband consume such a supper. While I am confident he would gladly eat those grits, I could not live with the guilt that something I made was not as good as it might have been.

So I took myself to Food City to avenge the Quaker's actions. I would find the corn grits ground by Bob's Red Mill. For though Bob's grits be yellow, I certainly am not. ◆

Black Pearl

ELIZABETH NOLL

When someone you love is dying, it should be fall. Things disappear one by one. Beauty is swollen with sadness. First the apples are done, all picked, the red skins all inside in a basket, leaving the tree with lonely pale green leaves, and those not long for this world either. The raspberries signal their waning days by clinging tightly to the white nipples, and they fill only the bottom of a small bowl rather than to the brim. Some have rotted or dried up on the cane. The sunflowers are brown and bent, stalks and flower both, with little glimpses, inches, fragments of yellow, like when a sister gets up and has a sparkle in her deep brown eyes, and she sits and watches a cooking show with you, before the cancer and the oxycodone drive her back to bed. Not to "oblivion" because it is not. Not yet.

Though we have lost much of her already—her rolling, hiccupping laugh, her chatter (since the cancer took her tongue, her speech is so slurred we don't understand her, mostly, and she has to write on a dry-erase board), her wild blueberry pie, her gifts for no reason, her funny stories of garage sale finds—we do still have her, and we cling to her even as we lose her, and we remember what we had: It is still there in our eyes and our hearts and on our tongues, the taste of her wild blueberry pie made two years ago, when she was still whole and the cancer was growing but nobody knew it yet. We have her and at the same time we see her failing and falling and moving into another season.

The cherry tomatoes are next, plenty green and pale orange turning on the vine but without enough time to ripen—not nearly enough time. The Chinese doctor said to her, "Your lifeline is longer than mine." My sister with the dark brown eyes turned them to me, and we saw both saw a pair of eyes with tears, and she said with a deep, relieved sigh, "Oh, good, then I have time." The frost comes, though, and crushes the cells in the leaves and turns the tomatoes to mush. The Chinese doctor was wrong.

The clove currants have leaves of stunning red creeping through veins to golden green palms. A tiny shiny black teardrop on a twig close to the ground glints in the sun, like the black pearls my sister bought at the Holland farmers market, a string of freshwater, to put on her neck below the four-by-four white square of gauze that covers a crater in her neck where the radiation burned away a cup of flesh, a yellow bowl that must be packed with a fresh dressing daily. Black tears, like black pearls, both surprising.

I eat one. It is sweet. It has seeds. I think of my son and I don't pick the rest because he should see where they came from. The stripped twig, the black round fruit holding on, holding on, holding on, till someone tastes its sweetness.

That last sparkling juicy bit of sweetness, catching the sun before it is over and there is no more. No more berries, no more time, nothing. ◆

Raclette

TONNO BISACCIO

It's best in the early evening. Maybe after a long walk up there, far beyond the noise and scents of the valley, along paths you've gone on many times before. They're never the same, those trails, changing from hour to hour as the light shifts, as the clouds bring shadow, as winter snow melts or a hot summer sun turns the rocks more golden or bright or gray or sugar-white. Then, before night comes with all that light above—the Milky Way; the clear sky you never get to see anymore unless you live up there or in the desert somewhere; the easy, sweet air; the bells of the Hérens cows somewhere off where you can't see—place some rocks in a circle and light some gathered wood as the sun just begins its dip for the night. Have a sip (or three) of the simple, satisfying, spiked tea from the glass bottle—it tastes better coming from there—once you've put the fingerling potatoes on to boil, and maybe begin to open your appetite with a tangy slice (or three) of dried meat or chunky, rustic salami.

Whether you are two or five or eight, it will be a deeply pleasing moment. You don't need many words. You'll each be feeling similar things, sitting tired and serene after the paced hike—you learn that quickly above the tree line, to pace yourself to the rhythm of your own breath. You adopt a mountain gait, weighted, where you know where you've put the soles of your shoes and look where you'll be placing them in the following steps.

Once the potatoes are cooked, take the pickled onions and open another bottle of Fendant, the one Emile or Davide or Richard made from the small patch of vines on the mountainside below. Then out comes the half round of cheese: raclette, a local one made from the milk of cows up high in their summer grazing grounds. The round has a potent scent of leaves and fertile soil and flowers, a mélange of odors waiting to come together wafting off its deep cream color, solid and heavy and rich. Set it down in front of the fire until a first layer begins to melt away. Lift the round and with a broad knife slush the melting, now harmonious, mix onto a plate, then slice gently back up the round for the slightly caramelized rind. Pass the plate to the first of you, who will grab a hot potato, slice it through and add a good bit of cheese, maybe grate some black pepper on top. The cheese and tuber dissolve as he chews, nourishing and generous, as if the mountain itself were giving him a quick massage, an approval of the day. Then he will sip the wine as the next plate comes for the next layer of bubbling, melted raclette.

Soon enough it'll be your turn. For now, you can wait with serene patience. Like the mountain. ◆

Things Left Behind

CLAIRE IBARRA

She had announced that she was leaving, to both of us, separately. She told my father with promises of coming back one day. To me, it was announced after I was caught cutting class when I was thirteen. I lounged with my friends on the couch, gorging on chocolate kisses dipped in peanut butter while watching an episode of *All My Children*. My mother said, "Come with me, we need to talk."

I slouched on the edge of the bed, thinking I was busted for skipping out of school. The banter and laughter of my friends came through the door, while she gazed at me. Her eyes softened with sympathy, but she didn't smile. I can't remember our conversation, except for her repeated assurance. "It's all for the best," she said.

It had happened before, when I was seven. There was yelling and screaming in the driveway. My dad, angry and protective, carried me into the house. I had watched from behind the screen door as my mom climbed into a red Jeep and drove away with another man. Confused by her sudden departure, I cried, while tugging at the frayed mesh on the door.

At that time, my father took me on a long camping trip to Big Sur. Our flight to the redwoods was meant to distract me and soothe his pain. And since my dad didn't tell my mom where we were going, it also served to punish her.

We ate meals at a small diner up the road from the campsite, or grilled hot dogs on the fire. He strummed flamenco on his classical guitar at the skirt of the forest, while my seven-year-old self jumped off boulders and twirled around and around, like Wonder Woman. If I was like Wonder Woman, then wasn't my father able to be a superhero, too?

Yet, my mother's announcement that she was leaving us again was not the defining moment. It came later, after she moved out the last of her things, and her closet and bathroom were left bare of her lacy vintage clothes, her jewelry, and her musky floral scent.

Months after she left, my father and I grew accustomed to a routine without her. I did my own laundry and walked to school. I spent as much time as I could at friends' homes. I ate meals at other families' tables or pizza out of the box. My father and I drifted through the house like spirits—bewildered, lost, and detached.

One evening I crept through the house. Wandering from my bedroom into the dimly lit kitchen, I stood for a few moments. The hum of the refrigerator was the only sign of life. Then my dad walked in.

"So, what shall we have for dinner?" Dad said, feigning cheer. He walked over to the refrigerator and opened it with wide eyes, as if a home-cooked meal would appear before him by magic. I stood beside him, and we stared at the expired carton of milk and the rotten iceberg lettuce. The refrigerator was a white cavern, barren and cold, and smelled spoiled and moldy.

The refrigerator was a reflection of our lives.

I froze. I watched my dad's shoulders fall and slouch. His head hung low and his eyes were downcast. He sobbed, and putting his arms around me, hugged me close, desperate and grasping for life.

My dad's vulnerability frightened me. As I stood in that cold and empty kitchen, I took a step back and told myself, "You have to take care of yourself."

My father came to visit recently. We worked in the kitchen together, beside my daughters. My father sautéed mushrooms in butter and wine. My daughters debated the health risks of genetically modified foods. I chopped garlic. We drank wine, my teenage girls stealing sips, and we listened to Santana.

"Can you get out the cilantro?" my dad asked.

I opened the refrigerator, filled with fruits and vegetables and containers of leftovers. The milk carton would not expire for two more weeks and the romaine lettuce was green and fresh. I held the cilantro to my nose and breathed in the sweet scent. Shutting the door, I closed my eyes. Then I rinsed the cilantro, placed it on the wood block, and began chopping the fine leaves. ◆

Ma'amouls and Nuns' Bellies

ANNE MCGOURAN

"The Ottoman Sultan's Men" exhibit occupied several display cases at the Royal Ontario Museum. Among the complex hierarchy of servants, chamberlains, and spies, one well-fed man in an inverted ice cream cone hat and embroidered tunic stood out: The Secretary of the Palace Sweetmeat Makers. When it sunk in that his only job was taste-testing halvah for imperial banquets, I felt cheated. My childhood Sunday dinners consisted of gristly meat and curdled milk pudding made with 1950s Junket Rennet Tablets. I fantasized about spun sugar bird's nests, buttercream gâteaux, and *îles flottantes* glimpsed in vintage cookbooks at the library.

A sweet tooth runs in my family. Humbugs, Eat a Yolks, Butlers Irish Toffee. Whenever his bedridden grandfather paid him to fetch a noggin of ale from the Crossroads public house, my Dad (age nine) would splurge on candy from County Down, Northern Ireland's only newsagent. He'd linger over apothecary jars full of fruit drops and nutty lumps and traipse home, pockets bulging with Yellowman, a chewy honeycomb toffee that tastes of burnt sugar. At Quebec sugar shack parties in the 1920s, my mother drizzled hot maple syrup in snow to make *tire sur la neige*. She squandered her pocket money on maple pralines and horehound drops from J. A. Moisan General Store. Her homemaker mother regularly dished out the Irish trinity for dinner: boiled cabbage, leathery beef, and mashed potatoes. And yet, on special occasions she somehow produced ethereal poached meringues on custard. (Boil milk, salt, and vanilla sugar, then simmer egg yolks and scalded milk. Carefully mold stiffened egg whites into balls, briefly suspend them in boiling water and float these poofy islands on a well-chilled custard sea.)

That kind of careful, time-consuming cooking is much less common these days. How I wish my grandmother had passed down her special occasion recipes to me! She died before I was born and my mother, ever dismissive of "kitchen arts," relied almost exclusively on packaged foods. From time to time I attempt a homemade dessert: clafoutis with damson plums baked in tiny ramekins. It's like a soufflé for cheaters ... puffy flan in the middle and cake around the edges. I'll even whip up a hybrid soda bread currant loaf but I have to talk myself through it as if Gran is whispering in my ear: "Stir in soured milk until you get craggy lumps. Lightly knead the dough."

At university, I gravitated to Kensington Market's Portuguese bakeries and their dizzying array of egg yolk sweets. *Pastéis de nata* (lemon-scented custard*)* and shattery-crisp *suspiros* (meringues like sighs). There were puddingy delicacies with religious names: *pão de Deus* (heavenly bread)*; pastéis de Santa Clara* (Saint Clare's pastries)*; barrigas de freira* (nun's bellies). The baker arranging egg tarts in Nova Era's pastry case repeated the same tired joke: "One minute on the lips ... a lifetime on the hips" whenever she slipped me a buttery *biscoito* for dunking in milky coffee.

During my gap year, I finally sampled Turkish sweets worthy of the Palace Sweetmeat Maker. I still have a photo of *Patisserie Du Sud Tunisien* on Rue de la Harpe in Paris's Latin Quarter. A navy-and-white awning ... sweets shaped like tiny cigars, leaves, snow cones, and pretzels. Hand to his heart, the owner assured me his homemade *asure* (dried fruit and nut-studded pudding) contained each of the forty ingredients left behind in Noah's Ark. I paid for my binge in sugar jitters. I skipped manically over Pont Saint-Michel, followed by an energy nosedive/early night at my overpriced pension.

My sweetness receptors have changed with age. Along with the hereditary *dent sucrée* came hypoglycemia. I still enjoy the occasional shortbread or fruit dessert but no more farmers market cinnamon buns, funnel cakes, or fried *churros*. No croquembouche, that sadistic cream puff tower glued together with caramel. Luckily, I can still visualize Rue de la Harpe ... those perfectly crimped Tunisian *ma'amoul* cookies on a three-tiered metal tray. Their buttery-sandy texture and intricate shapes: slightly flattened for date; round for walnut; oval for pistachio.

Breaking news: A local Syrian family now offers authentic *knafeh* (melted white cheese in phyllo dough sprinkled with pistachios). The drizzle of orange blossom syrup on crispy pastry takes mouthfeel to a whole new level. I'm already putty in their hands. ◆

Making Sherry Eat

SHERRY POFF

I sat silently in the dimly lit lunchroom watching the chicken gravy and peas on my school lunch tray cool and glaze over. I could hear laughter and shouts from my first-grade classmates out on the playground. I could go outside, I was told, when I had eaten my lunch.

I had never been forced to eat anything. My mother operated on a rule handed down from her father: If you have to make children eat, it doesn't do them any good. I had led a very happy existence at home for nearly six years before entering school, cheerily eating oatmeal and my mother's big puffy biscuits for breakfast, peanut butter crackers for snacks, and beans, potatoes, and cornbread for supper.

In the summer, Mom let me have all the fresh lettuce I wanted and baked plenty of crunchy cornbread to eat with green onions and sliced tomatoes. She took me to the garden to pick corn and cucumbers, and then let me help string and break green beans, which I ate with enthusiasm. Whenever we got a watermelon, Daddy cut it into big, plate-sized slices and sprinkled salt on top. I slurped it up. There were many foods I loved. Chicken gravy, however, was something I would not like to try, and canned peas smelled funny.

So there I sat day after day, my dark head bowed over the lunch tray, close-mouthed and glum. I knew the routine. When the bell rang signaling the end of recess, I would be allowed to empty my plate and go to class, where Mrs. Williams would sigh over me in exasperation and turn to write on the board.

One fateful day, in complete frustration I suppose, Mrs. Williams stopped me on my way to the large gray trash cans where I would rake out my plate. Grabbing my fork, she scooped up some spaghetti and pointed it at my mouth. I was stubborn, but not usually disobedient, and she had caught me off guard. Without thinking, I opened my mouth and in went the spaghetti, now cold and slimy from sitting on my plate for nearly an hour. In a very few seconds, the spaghetti came out again, and with it what was left of my biscuits and oatmeal. Mrs. Williams grabbed my plate. "Go to the bathroom," she barked.

On the bus ride home I thought about it again: the slimy spaghetti hitting my tongue, the sudden warmth rising from my stomach, and Mrs. Williams' look of horror and disgust. I told the story to my mom at home, getting ready for bed. She didn't have a lot to say, just some questions as she poured hot water from a steaming kettle into the big round tub for my bath: "What happened then? Did you go to class? How do you feel now?"

In just a few days, there was an open house at school. The dreaded lunchroom was transformed into a meeting hall. A stage at one end provided a platform for programs and speakers. After hearing us sing "Smokey the Bear" and recite Joyce Kilmer's "Trees," parents were dismissed to classrooms where they met with our teachers. Mom and I looked around the room, oddly unfamiliar in the evening. We found my desk, and I showed off my colored pictures and handwriting samples. Then it was Mom's turn to talk with Mrs. Williams. After only a minute or two, we were ready to go.

I rode the bus to school the next day, just like always. I wrote in my writing pad with my fat red pencil, just like always; went to the bathroom in a line to wash my hands before lunch, and picked up my tray from the counter by the kitchen, just like always. When I sat down with my food, I ate the warm, yeasty roll that I enjoyed, stirred my mashed potatoes, and even sampled a few bites, but when the time came to leave, no one held me back. I raked my uneaten lunch into the trash can and ran up the stairs and out into the sunshine with the rest of my class. My mother—my beautiful, wise mother—had been to school and had left clear instructions for everyone: "Do not try to make Sherry eat." ◆

A Meal in Venice

DARYL SCROGGINS

My friends Rick and Teel Sale, both writers and artists, lived a few blocks away from the university where they taught for many years and where I was teaching. The many fine home-cooked meals they invited me to there made the hours between my day classes and evening classes the best part of each week, and I will never forget the conversations we had. They never ran out of amazing stories. One evening our talk turned to favorite meals in faraway places, and Teel conjured one in an instant that must have remained brightly detailed in her memory for years, as it has remained in mine.

They were in Venice in 1978 and decided to walk around one late afternoon to find a place to eat dinner. They had heard tales of wonderful seafood to be had in Venice, but had so far found it far too expensive in the restaurants they visited. They walked down narrow streets and discovered a small café. Above it was an apartment balcony covered with night-blooming flowers. They went in and saw the place had only four tables and a bar. A boy sat at a table playing chess with a sailor—beating him soundly by the looks of it—and another sailor sat drinking and reading a newspaper at the bar. The owner came out, a short but large man, balding, wearing a rather soiled white apron. Teel asked him if he made a fish soup. The man paused, and then asked how long they could wait for it. Rick and Teel told him as long as it took, they were in no hurry. He returned to the kitchen, and soon a boy brought wine and bread to the table. Then the owner emerged from the kitchen, having shed his apron, carrying a large basket. He nodded at Rick and Teel, and walked briskly out of the restaurant.

The owner returned in about half an hour with a huge fish overlapping both sides of his basket, which also contained a mass of greens and several bags of clams and shrimp and other ingredients. This he took to the kitchen, and soon the most wonderful smell wafted out to the diners. The owner's sons (one of them the chess player) and wife all hovered at the kitchen door, cooing sounds of delight. After a while the owner came out with a great platter—the fish cooked whole on the greens—and a large bowl of freshly made fish stock. The kids followed him, all saying, "Papa! Papa, you did it! You made it!" He cut portions of the fish and put them in shallow bowls, then spooned broth over them. It was astonishingly good.

Rick and Teel's portions had scarcely made a mark in the great fish's bulk. Soon neighbors trickled in, drawn by the aroma, and the owner served family and friends from the platter, pouring wine for all, adding broth to bowls, bringing more bread. He even brought out a bottle of brandy he had made himself and poured small glasses all around. Rick and Teel had a wonderful time, but began to worry a bit about the cost, which hadn't been mentioned. Then the owner brought the bill: six dollars. They said it occurred to them later that the place was probably more of a bar than a restaurant, set up for a usual fare of light meals. But something had inspired the owner on this night. I asked Rick and Teel if they thought the man's soup was something he had made in the past, in another place, and perhaps he thought they had heard of it and had sought him out specifically for that reason. But they didn't know.

Now, when I think of fine meals with friends, this meal comes to mind as one of my own. ◆

Waiting for Marshmallows

DEBORAH THOMPSON

I have a vivid recollection of taking the marshmallow test when I was a child. You must have read about that famous, infamous, 1970s test. The child can eat the marshmallow before her, or she can wait for fifteen minutes and then get two. Her choice was supposed to predict later success in life. Greater self-control meant more success, was the hypothesis.

I remember the saliva flowing molten in my mouth. The whiff of perfect sweet nothingness before me; my tongue feeling restlessly for that squishy, foamy, comforting air pillow; the whiteness of the puff; the promise of fulfillment.

That was back when eating was still fun; back before I knew about calories and counting; before I pinched my waist, or winced when my thighs touched; before I discovered that female flesh was a trap; before I learned to transvalue hunger and turn it into a virtue; before I called food a four-letter word.

The marshmallow test was never well controlled, and bore an implicit bias toward justifying meritocracy: kids who can resist instant gratification succeed, and those who lack self-control can't. The test didn't account for class or race, or for how kids from food-insecure families might not trust the promises of an authority figure and might know better than to let a good marshmallow go to waste. Nor did it challenge the accepted notion of success. While the test was flawed, though, I bought into its ideology. Pleasure is not to be had, but to be anticipated.

They should have investigated the marshmallow test as a predictor for eating disorders. How well can you taunt your tongue? How good are you at playing mind games with your body? Can you learn to savor hunger itself? Can you learn to imagine the fairy-light sugar cloud on your tongue without actually sensing it? Can you eat with your mind only? Will you come to regard all food as that promised marshmallow?

Even though my memory is so vivid, it's unlikely that I ever actually took the marshmallow test as a child. Perhaps my mother improvised her own version of it. A sociology major and amateur sleuth of the psyche, she might have devised a version for my brother and me. It's possible. I have no doubt that my brother, hyperactive and learning disabled, would have eaten the confection immediately. I have no doubt that I would have waited.

Although I say I have vivid memories of taking the test, that's only partially true. I have vivid memories of waiting, of swallowing saliva, of breathing in the sweet smell of marshmallow that has no smell outside of imagination. I have no memory of finally getting that second marshmallow, or even the first. No memory of finally touching my tongue to its powdery starchy sweet surface, though I almost surely would have licked it first before biting. I don't remember teeth chewing squishing melting oozing. I remember only waiting. ◆

Kuidaore: A Taste of Japan

RENÉE COHEN

Over dinner in a local French bistro, my partner asked me, "If you could go anywhere in the world, where would you want to go?"

"Japan," I replied without hesitation.

Shortly thereafter, that dream became a reality.

In retrospect, I realize that my favorite memories of that month-long trip are primarily food related. For thirty days we enjoyed authentic Japanese meals, sampling local fare three times a day in a variety of restaurants (in addition to continually munching on snacks to fuel our daily meanderings).

My knowledge of Japanese is minimal, but one word in particular intrigued me: *kuidaore*. Apparently, a rough translation of the word means to bring ruin on oneself through eating. While the word originated in Osaka, a town famous for its food—and foodies—I learned about it perusing a copy of *The World's Leading Hotels* found on the desktop of our Tokyo hotel suite.

While the idea of bringing on "ruination" through eating seemed like a fun and decadent goal, though not for our lack of trying, our daily food binges didn't manage to ruin us physically. (Monetarily might be a different story.)

I admit that on more than one occasion, an exquisite Japanese meal was undermined by a bean-filled mochi or some equally unappealing, tasteless dessert. The frequently sad Japanese desserts left me pining for sweeter concoctions (preferably devoid of beans).

Despite that tiny hiccup, the majority of our Japanese dining experiences were awe-inspiring. Largely composed of multitudes of small servings, meals were both copious and humbling. Up until that trip, I had always considered myself to be knowledgeable about food, yet many of the items we'd eaten in Japan had been entirely unfamiliar. The experience of the unknown was a valuable learning experience.

The closest we came to physically experiencing *kuidaore* didn't occur when we were visiting Osaka, but when we had our first *kaiseki* meal at our *ryokan* (traditional inn) in Kyoto. The culinary experience of over thirteen dishes was an esthetically beautiful feast—for the eyes and the palate.

At the low dining table of our open concept suite, we sat on the floor with our backs propped up against tapestry-covered, legless chair backs shaped like bookends.

The meal was prefaced by a velvety plum wine, the first serving of which was poured from the decanter into my partner's cup by our server, Sanae.

The plum wine was followed by tender pieces of fresh crab adorned with delicate, pastel-colored flowers set on a plate dotted with gingko beans. Again, Sanae served my partner first. Her natural inclination to serve the man first was a subtle reminder that we were visiting a traditionally patriarchal society. I realized then that being served first was something I had always taken for granted.

Pacific saury fish, or *samna*, was proceeded by miso soup that contained cloud mushrooms and sea urchins. Pickled barracuda plated with purple radish leaves and salmon roe followed. Next, zaba sushi—the flattened mackerel specialty of Kyoto—was served alongside two walnut halves and a two-inch-long ginger stem that was partly colored red. Correctly assuming we wouldn't know any better, Sanae graciously warned us that the red half was not edible. Had she remained silent we certainly would have eaten it, or at least tried to.

The *kaiseki* dinner continued for hours, filled with intriguing delicacies, each dish more inspired than the previous. Until dessert. Our memorable and refined *kaiseki* feast ended with a gross orange blob of something resembling Jell-O. Had we eaten it, "ruination" likely would have ensued.

We recently revisited the French bistro where we had initially discussed visiting Japan. Over a heavy starter of escargots covered with cream sauce, a stark contrast to Japanese cuisine, we reminisced about our visits to the bamboo forest, many temples and parks, museums, and the courtesy of all commuters on the Japanese subway system.

When the waitress brought our second course to the table, I suggested that, in homage to Japanese custom, she serve my partner first.

"But only this time:... and only because it's his birthday," I added.

After I too had been served, I asked my partner, "If you could go anywhere in the world, where would you want to go?" ◆

Food Evolution: From the Mountains to the Mississippi

ROBERT KING

Anyone who eats should write about food. Language is nurturing, words have calories, and sentences energize; ideas give meaning to our lives.

I reviewed restaurants for fifteen years, and it's a recommended way for learning your city and the cultures with which you coexist—immigration patterns, for example. An ethnic restaurant serves as a traditional way for immigrants to start a business and survive in a strange land—language is less of a commercial barrier; home-cooking basics from Thailand or Mexico or Vietnam can please the Anglo palate; family provides cheap labor; the restaurant feeds your family and fellow immigrants. It is one of the many proven virtues of immigration.

Writing about the restaurant scene engages you with creative, energetic, and oral folks. A generation or two into the past century, the chef stereotype resembled more a tattooed short-order cook, semi-literate at best, and likely on drugs. Chefs now function as a serious part of our celebrity-digital-cable TV culture. And, for better or worse, restaurants are a high-profile battleground for the #MeToo movement and racial integration. Culinary kitchen talent may be more color-blind than sports.

And writing about restaurants made my institutional, academic day job seem sane.

When I arrived in Salt Lake City in 1977, at the age of twenty-eight, there were no coffeehouses or fresh fish to be found. Outside of a few decent diners, the options were a half-dozen "Chinese" restaurants that seemed to have the same central Cantonese kitchen, or 3.2 beer in smoky pubs. No worthy crusty bread existed except for the sourdough at Finn's restaurant and Beehive rye. Don't even ask about bagels.

A rising tide raises all boats, even on the Great Salt Lake. A more discerning American culinary scene emerged due to European travel, changes in immigration laws, availability of products, local sourcing, and creative and energetic chefs. Connoisseurship has its costs, but also its rewards—in Salt Lake, The Bagel Project offers a good place to *schmear* cream cheese for a proper communion; fresh fish flies into Salt Lake's airport daily and sushi abounds; we know now that there is a North and a South to Italy (see or see again the film *Big Night*) and that China has distinctive regional cuisines. Thousands swarm Salt Lake's Great Yuppie Reunion, the Saturday morning downtown farmers market.

Through writing and inquiry, I learned there are two general rules in American restaurants: 1) family- and chef-owned restaurants give a city's dining its character, its backbone; and 2) what citizens will pay for an ethnic dinner reflects roughly that ethnic group's status in the social hierarchy—French, Northern Italian, Japanese on the one hand; Mexican, Chinese, soul food on the other.

Of course, there are exceptions and evolutionary changes to the second rule, and the elevation of Creole, Cajun, and African American cuisines in New Orleans contradicts the rule—the cuisines of the swamps and slave quarters are served up in the city's white-tablecloth restaurants. (This is perhaps an abrupt shift from Salt Lake to New Orleans, but the cities have their NBA Jazz connection—the Jazz moved from New Orleans to Salt Lake City in 1979. Many a jokester has remarked that New Orleans' NFL Saints would be a more apt choice for Mormon Utah.)

Living in New Orleans has its challenges during hurricane season, but its distinctive, expressive history makes it easy and attractive to write about food, e.g., Sara Roahen's *Gumbo Tales: Finding My Place at the New Orleans Table* (2008). At the renowned, and relatively expensive, family-owned restaurants—Galatoire's, Arnaud's, the Brennan's several outposts, for example—gumbos and "dirty" rice and beans and crawfish étouffée come at a premium. The elevation of these humbly sourced cuisines reflects that unique aspect of New Orleans—the expressive cultures of its oppressed minorities found a place at the table, perhaps with a locally sourced jazz trio in the background.

Whether it's Salt Lake or New Orleans or your own home turf, to know a city's restaurant history and culture is a tasteful mode of engagement and expression, of finding meaning and understanding. Or gather stories at the farmers market. For indeed, we are what we eat. ◆

The Sausage Stuffing

TINA TOCCO

We missed the sausage stuffing that year because my grandpa wanted to give me some fruit.

In 1978, my grandpa spent the last two weeks of November in St. John's Riverside Hospital in Yonkers, New York. I was just on my way to turning five and a half. My mom and grandma—and maybe my grandpa, too—were on their way to realizing that Thanksgiving was the last Thanksgiving they'd remember all of us in our vintage Yonkers apartment.

I can't remember any of those Thanksgivings. Or this one. But I know my mom, grandma, and uncle took me back to St. John's Riverside for the first time since I'd been born there. And I know we went that day because the nurses in the terminal wards had brought the patients little bowls of fruit. And I know my grandpa wanted to share his fruit with me, and that he gave me some red grapes even though he knew someone would have to help me with the seeds.

And even though I can't remember, we sat in a booth in a diner in a town called Hastings for the rest of the afternoon, my uncle having driven all the way up from his job in Bethesda like any Thanksgiving. So I imagine myself as my mom describes me on any Thanksgiving, keeping a lookout for early snow, but this time on a street that wasn't ours, through windows that were clean but not home-clean, my nose close to the corner where soap bubbles had settled and popped and dirtied themselves. And when I finally grow up, and finally ask about that afternoon, my mom says that, like any Thanksgiving, we ate turkey and some sort of vegetable and whatever else someone stacked on our plates. But not the stuffing.

My family's sausage stuffing is exactly as it sounds. It's as meaty as any turkey, and as common at our Thanksgiving dinner as sweet potatoes or lasagna. It's like goop under your nails when you're making it, like steam on your cheeks when it's scooped out of the bird, and like breakfast when you get it in your mouth. Chestnuts, cranberries, apples, figs, and all other manner of potpourri are proudly absent.

But that year—just that one year—the stuffing was absent. After cooking three generations of Thanksgivings—breaking sausage at her gas stove, the onions minced and then melted, her housecoat sopping up snaps of oil— my grandma ate turkey but no stuffing. My grandma, who would only give up her wedding ring to arthritis, sat in a diner with soap on the windows because my grandpa wanted to give me some fruit. ◆

Cookie Monster

CHERISE BENTON

Spend the afternoon doing errands with your mother instead of dating your Tim. Start by buying a quarter pound of each bacon flavor except for "Elvis," because both peanut butter and bananas are gross and make your throat feel like anaphylaxis is setting in. You buy all of the food at the supermarket.

You get home fourteen hours after leaving. You warm up Goya brand frozen delicacies and Totino's pizza rolls.

Ask your Tim very nicely to stop talking long enough for you to press failed shortbread cookie dough into a pie pan, and then to make himself useful by crushing Oreos into it.

Soften an outrageous spoonful of Biscoff cookie butter in the microwave. Drizzle it over the Oreo mess. You lick the word "drizzle" while it's on your tongue. Smash the rest of the dough on top, pop it in the oven, eat the warm snacks, and watch a movie.

Eventually the cookie thing is baked and you eat it with ice cream until you want to die.

The next morning you wake up at a responsible hour and realize you passed out at 10:30 last night from a cookie overdose. And stayed asleep.

You weep for your squandered youth. You could have had beautiful cocktails with beautiful people, but you chose to eat as many cookies as you could until someone told you to cut it out.

A few days ago, your good friend's mom gave you jars of her homemade preserves. By now you have stumbled down the stairs to your kitchen because you nearly broke your toe doing a handstand the night you received the jam. It was excitement. Celebration. Inebriation. Whatever.

Peach cobbler preserves catalyze something in your heart. You make your Tim pick which bacon he would like to taste in the grilled cheese. Paprika is off-limits because that is for your grandmother's potato soup you're going to make her this afternoon. He selects country cured. You fry it.

You slice onions. You cook them in bacon fat.

You spread the preserves on the multigrain bread you picked out for Tim. Tim loves toast. Especially multigrain toast.

Neil deGrasse Tyson is on the Nerdist Podcast while you're doing all of these things.

You unwrap the regular mozzarella cheese and attempt to slice it. You pile the irregular strips onto the jammed bread and wonder when your free-hand cheese-slicing skills will realize.

The onions are ready! Smother the cheese with them.

One quarter pound of bacon from the meat shop is exactly four slices. You realize you will only get to taste this exact sandwich once because the ratio of sandwich to bacon is always one sandwich to two slices of bacon. So it goes.

There's enough bacon grease left after the onions to fry two eggs. So you do, and poorly butter the outer slices of the sandwiches as the eggs lose their dippy quality, which is fine, because this sandwich is already dangerously juicy.

Everything is finally ready. You lift the first sandwich toward the hot, dry pan and it falls completely apart. You are a failure. Tim says that NDT had just said you figured out a way not to make that sandwich. You ignore him to concentrate on scowling and pouting.

The. Sandwich. Is. Glorious.

You eat it all, just like the cookie from the night before; you know you should chew mindfully, but if you eat it faster, you will have *tasted the whole thing* before your infarction sets in.

You can't turn your head because the arteries in your neck are already clogged. You don't care because: eat well, die young. You are living one of your mantras. Your Tim is basically crying at the beauty that used to be on his plate and can't get the last bite of his sandwich into his face. You are a champion.

You photograph the remains so you can brag on the Internet. And so that you never forget peach cobbler preserves with country-cured bacon, cara-melized onions, and mozzarella cheese. *Before noon.* Because you died the cookie death of a warrior Viking princess the night before, before the bars even got full. ◆

Two Sides of the Same Buffet

SHEILA S. HUDSON

"Sorry your mother died. Here's a ham." That's a greeting I've heard since childhood. In the Deep South, funerals and weddings are two sides of the same buffet.

As a child, I said, "Mom, I don't like funerals." She replied, "What's to like? Any decent Southern woman knows you take potato salad or a home-made pie to the house, you sign the guest book, and you go to the services. You hug your great aunts, shake hands with cousins you've never met, and wear clean underwear. Do you want to embarrass me in front of the whole town?"

With that tender admonition, I embraced the world of food, customs, and Southern tradition. Etiquette for weddings is basically the same as for funerals. The only difference is that wedding food is catered in—well, most of the time. I had a cousin who assigned what you were to bring to the reception printed on the invitation. She, however, was on my father's side of the family and that's another story.

Weddings, funerals, and their distant cousin—family reunions—bring out the relatives you don't get to see, don't want to see, don't know, and perhaps would rather forget.

Every child has heard "Look how you've grown," and "You look just like [insert another family member's name here]." These people are your blood relatives, yet you only see them in times of greatest stress and then you need a name tag.

I have a theory that a non-family member could crash one of these events by simply picking up a plate in the buffet line and claiming they are Aunt Mary's offspring. Everyone has an Aunt Mary. If you were vague enough about details, a slick operator hungry for banana pudding could pull it off and garner a few invitations for Sunday dinner in the bargain. The reason an imposter could hoodwink himself elbow-deep into the bread pudding is that family reunion attendees are terrible at introducing each other. Sure, the patriarchs know the crowd and they assume everyone else does too. We, the sons and daughters of the patriarchs, stand around feeling awkward but too embarrassed to introduce ourselves or ask a cousin his first name.

That's the real value of the barbecue or the buffet. Food is the universal icebreaker. When all else fails, food is the remedy. Food is the glue of Southern heritage.

When someone dies, you take an entire meal to the deceased's kinfolks. Tradition demands that it contain fried chicken, heavily battered and accompanied with healthy green beans swimming in fatback, and new potatoes. If this isn't enough cholesterol to stop your heart, top it off with cornbread and biscuits dripping with freshly churned sweet butter. A ham or turkey could substitute in a pinch, but not as well. Southern women intent upon presenting their wares then uncover their pièce de résistance: a pecan pie, sweet potato pie, or freshly grated coconut cake. Neighbors with less time to bake might offer assorted tarts, tea cakes, and homemade shortbread. Southern men don't have strokes for nothing.

Weddings bring with them the traditional finger foods, with the bride's wedding cake and the groom's cake. Pigs in a blanket, buffalo wings, and cold cuts are perennial favorites as long as barbecue sauce flows like wine.

Reunion meals run neck-in-neck to funeral carry-in fare, except these dinners are traditionally eaten outside. When I was growing up, no church allowed you to eat indoors. Farsighted church leaders hadn't installed bathrooms yet, much less kitchens or, God forbid, fellowship halls. The host matriarch of the church carefully supervised "dinner on the grounds." She was easy to spot by her wrestler stance at the center of the main table, poised with a paper plate in each hand. With the grace of a ballerina in perfect cadence, she discouraged yellow jackets from landing on the uncovered casseroles, salads, and main dishes spread like sacrifices on sacred stone tables.

Southern food aromas bring the best memories of all. While vacationing in Hawaii, Sugar and I were guests at a traditional luau. "Luau" is just Hawaiian for "buffet." When asked how he liked it, my mate replied, "Just one suggestion. Bring your own barbecue sauce."

Mama always said, "You can dress him up but you can't take him anywhere." Not even to a funeral. ◆

Dear Erik

BRIAN PHILLIP WHALEN

My friend, how many more occasions have we left in our steeply narrowing lives to brood over decisions like these? To write, to teach—to marry. It used to be we'd sit in bars at 3 a.m. speculating cream versus half-and-half, debating French press versus good espresso, with the same intensity with which we argued Carlyle versus Wordsworth (all brazen and floral and thirsty for truths).

Do you remember a morning in your kitchen, in Asheville, the year after your mother died? You brewed Ethiopian Yirgacheffe while Heidi made us omelets stuffed with braised chard from her garden. We spoke of poetry and lesson plans as Heidi beat eggs with salt and heated a pan. The smell of browned butter returned me, as always, to our grad school days, and that cottage in Virginia where you taught me to make kasha. You had all kinds of teas on those cottage shelves, Cyrillic names on the wrappers, gifts left over from the wild-hearted Russian girl you dated, the one who prompted you to tell me I was too meek to handle a mail-order bride. You showed me, in detail, the proper way to toast the buckwheat, to scramble the eggs with garlic in butter, to warm the stock, all while telling me about a girl—not the Russian—who climbed in your bedroom window late one night, uninvited; and how you broke it off with her, the intruder, before sunrise (you'd chosen that cottage, after all, for the freedom it offered, in solitude).

How many women did we talk about, over the years, in that cottage, or downtown, hungover, at brunch in The Little Grille, where you'd steal dollops of crema off my huevos rancheros while we sparred over Romantic aesthetics? It was there, over coffee and eggs, we first shared stories of love and disaster: my sister—and her drug addiction; your sister—and her newborn child; my college girlfriend—how she ruined my head; your college girlfriend—how she ruined your heart, how she booted you out of the NYC apartment you leased together, how you rode in circles on the subway until dawn, with nothing but a gym bag of clothes and your cat, Leon, in his kennel beside you (Leon, fiery proud, prowler of field mice, by your side through it all, until the day his forepaw got snagged in a trapper's steel jaw—and the vet put him down).

We had all the time in the world back then; all the cream, served in metal *saucières*, that our hearts desired.

Ten years later, in Asheville, on your neighborhood street—with a mortgage to pay, and hens in your yard, and Heidi's plants in the garden, green and fulsome alongside your herbs—you were yet to propose (that secret part of you still clinging to freedom, still cleft-hooved and wild, windows latched). I watched you grind beans by hand in a cast-iron mill while Heidi plated our omelets. The water for the press pot was not boiling; you were, as always, too soon to take it off the burner. The result, I knew, would be a weak brew, too timidly steeped. I'd a mind to admonish, to argue technique, but as Heidi laid out mugs with unimpugnable devotion, I only loved you as I watched you pour the water over the grounds, ready the plunger—and wait. ◆

Consonance of Akko

JENNIFER LANG

Ramparts: **Philippe and I stroll** along Old City walls, remnants from once-upon-a-time rulers under the Byzantines, Crusaders, Ottomans, et cetera. A deeply tanned teenager springs onto the ledge and scans sailboats docked in the port, container ships bound for Haifa, and the Mediterranean Sea taking a nap. He shouts in Arabic to a bobbing body below. Israeli Jewish children in identical youth-group caps stare, pointing at the boy in the water and screaming in Hebrew, "*Tistakel, tistakel*!" ("Look, look!") We follow their fingers and squeeze hands. The ledge boy dives headfirst. The kids hoot. My stomach somersaults.

Fish restaurant: At Uri Buri, we order the tasting menu for two. Mushroom bisque whets our palate before a passel of small plates arrives, carrying fish with undecipherable names—*forel, lavrak, locus, musht, sandal*. One served with wasabi sorbet, one with coconut milk and apples, one with caramel and cubed beetroots. We *ooh* and *aah*. Our waitress reminds us to tell her *dai* when we've had enough. We want more. Hunks of rare, tender tuna bathing in yogurt and fiery red chili slices thrill our taste buds. Uri enters, his round face and Santa Claus beard easy to spot. "Looks like God," I giggle.

Cats: As we zig and zag under arches and through crooked passageways, street cats scurry and scrounge for scraps. Every corner we turn, we inhale their sour piss as they glare at us—the trespassers. We pass doorways and domes, castles and churches, synagogues and mosques with names that make my tongue careen: Al-Jazzar, Al-Majadalah, El-Bahar, El-Zeituna. A tin-tinnabulation echoes through the alleys, perhaps Maronites or Franciscans, Latin Catholic or Greek Orthodox. A concert of sounds, consonance of belief, harmony of culture. People—be they Jews, Muslims, Christians, Druze or Baha'is—breathe together. The Old City of Akko screams ancient, exotic, intriguing. It wakes me up like a foreign country even though it's only ninety minutes north of us near Tel Aviv.

B&B: Deep asleep in a cocoon of darkness, I hear it. The muezzin's call to prayer penetrates through window, walls, even earplugs.

Falafel: Friday afternoon frenzy, hours before sundown—Shabbat—we stand in line, instructed to tell anyone else who arrives *zeho,* no more. We're last. The one-man falafel maker frantically fills his utensil with the cumin-infused mixture: scoop, twirl, smooth, eject, scoop, twirl, smooth, eject. He repeats ten-fifteen-twenty times until dozens of globes sizzle in the large square vat. I watch, mesmerized by the movement. The April afternoon sun pounds our backs. My belly, empty after yesterday's feast and this morning's hike in the Western Galilee hills, rumbles.

Boat: We peer over the railing of the red-painted vessel. The port is lit like a scene from *The Arabian Nights*. Speedboats and yachts arrive and depart. A teal green mosque and matching skinny minaret dominate the foreground amid centuries-old stone structures. The captain plays brash Arabic music. Women in hijabs, heels, and jeans embark. Men with white caps and women in monochrome kaftans hold children in their laps. A school girl with eyes like molasses stares at my husband and me, the token Jews.

Souk: Along the sand-colored cobblestone passage, butchers sell next to fishmongers next to produce vendors next to bakeries with baklava and *basbousa* and *knafeh* next to spice sellers and coffee grinders next to touristy tchotchke stands. We enter Hummus Said, an unassuming restaurant in the middle of the market with a 4.5-star TripAdvisor rating. A half-dozen sweaty men chop, dice, soak, stir, mash, grind, and fry at a frenetic pace. Diners clasp hot, puffy pita in lieu of silverware, half-circling their wrists in an artful wipe—*lenagev*—around the chickpea spread. A movement I have yet to master, even after seven years in this country. Usually I feel self-conscious, stamped *other*. But here, now, on high alert, I embrace it. "Hungry?" Philippe asks. "*Yalla!*" I say, Arabic and Hebrew for "let's go," and we order. ◈

Something Fishy

LORI FONTANES

A few years ago I learned something about the man I married although we're no longer married and I didn't know what I'd learned until much later. Sometimes you have to work hard for knowledge. Sometimes it hits you like hour fourteen on the keto diet.

I'd spent that afternoon working on the miniature farm in the backyard we'd wrested from squirrels and lawn product salesmen. Deciding to grow anything other than arborvitae or hydrangea had made our home a neighborhood curiosity. We lived in the kind of New York town that boasts slim women in white jeans (summer) or pricey Canadian puffy coats (winter). Many residents never set foot in their gardens; I lived in mine. Through trial and much error, I'd learned how to raise forty different kinds of food, from tiny herbs to towering corn, and some of it the groundhogs even let us eat.

On that August day, the farm had kept me busier than usual. By the time I'd finished collecting tomatoes, chasing rodents, checking on seedlings, and plucking weeds, I realized it must be close to dinner. I had not actually made any dinner. A quick glance confirmed it was half an hour before my husband should be home. That's one thing about living in suburban New York. There are trains and schedules and people can plan a specific time to eat.

Best laid plans.

In this same moment, I also realized how hungry I was and decided that even though I was supposed to be all about food growing and home cooking, I was too tired to cook after spending the day growing. Since my husband had seemed extra preoccupied of late, I decided to splurge on sushi from our favorite place. That way we could have a nice meal together and maybe even talk.

He burst in from the garage already on his iPhone and didn't look up as he dropped his briefcase on the floor. I knew better than to bother him in the middle of a high-stakes e-mail so I waited until he was finished poking at the screen to tell him I'd ordered sushi. As I opened the door to return to the garden, I mentioned that I'd get our food as soon as I finished one last chore.

Then I went to the restaurant.

The cashier gave me a blank look when I asked for the order of sushi. She said there was no order of sushi. A rapid-fire discussion in Japanese between the cashier and the manager ensued. Did someone waltz off with my tuna naruto and crunchy salmon roll? That stuff is expensive!

The staff apologized and assured me they would make a new order. By this point, I was famished and would rather have gone home and reheated leftovers, but they were so apologetic I couldn't say no.

To take my mind off my stomach, I ran an errand. I returned to discover the staff was still upset—sushi-grade fish is expensive!—and they told me they thought a tall, blonde woman might have taken our food. At that point I remembered my car was in short-term parking so I moved it and came back.

They were still talking about the missing order. Did the woman—a long-time customer—take it by mistake? Or, cue sinister music, *on purpose*?

Eventually, I left with my bag of sushi.

Back home, I found my husband on the couch.

"Sushi!" I announced.

He looked at me. "Sushi?"

"Yeah, you wouldn't believe what happened!" I said as I unpacked my haul. "Some tall, blonde woman took our sushi and they had to make another order. Sorry it took so long!"

He stared at me. "But I already picked up the sushi."

"What?!"

He doesn't look anything like a tall, blonde woman, by the way.

"You told me you ordered sushi and I saw how busy you were so I drove over to get it."

Huh. Did not see that coming.

After a phone call to reassure the restaurant that we paid for both orders and, yes, that certainly was a lot of sushi but not to worry! No one walked off with any food.

I sat down to eat alone since the man I'd married had already eaten. But as hungry as I'd been, I couldn't finish it all. I suggested he save the leftovers to snack on later.

My husband shook his head. "I don't think so."

"Why not?" I demanded. "It'll go bad and that stuff is expensive!"

"I had sushi for lunch." ◆

Root Beer Popsicles and the Sick Sofa

REBECCA BEARDSALL

Root beer, like many drinks, has medicinal origins. Originally alcoholic, this beverage of berries, herbs, and bark was a social drink for early American settlers, an herbal home brew of sorts. This explains the drink's East Coast dominance. Charles Hires, a pharmacist in Philadelphia, started selling a medicinal, herbal tea of twenty-five different herbs, berries, and bark. He later turned the tea into a liquid concentrate and introduced commercial root beer to the public in 1876 at the Philadelphia Centennial Exhibition. In 1893 Hires began selling bottled versions of root beer.

I grew up an hour north of Philadelphia. Root beer, a staple sweet treat, is part of my history. Not only the drink, but root beer-flavored hard candy barrels and sticks, lollipops, licorice, and popsicles.

Root beer popsicles are rare, but they do exist. Popsicles—icy, throat-cooling treats—float me back to my childhood. As a kid I had many bouts of strep throat. A fever and a firebomb throat meant only one thing: a sheet-covered sofa and snuggles under the crocheted afghan, multiple hues of blue tucked under my chin, and copious quantities of popsicles.

In our house, a sheet draped over the sofa indicated either a day home from school with cartoons, or a sick sibling to stay away from. A tray table set up next to the sofa with water, medication, thermometer, and a small bell to ring during an emergency. A white basin on the tray table if an upset stomach was part of the problem. The sick sofa made it easier for Mom to keep an eye on us and also added the distraction of the television: *Sesame Street, Captain Kangaroo, The Electric Company, Captain Noah, Mister Rogers' Neighborhood.*

Strep throat, my childhood nemesis, came to visit a few times each year. Tonsil removal was an ongoing discussion, but never an action item. My relief came in the form of popsicles.

Bright, colorful, summer scenes, and smiling cartoon boxes of popsicles stacked in the upstairs freezer as I wallow on the sick sofa. Mom brings out the box and a bowl. She serves popsicles in a bowl to save the furniture, carpet, and clothing from dropped pieces and brightly colored drips.

"What flavor do you want?"

"Root beer."

"They didn't have root beer. We have orange, cherry, or grape."

"I want root beer."

"We have orange, cherry, or grape."

"Grape." A dramatic concession with full pout and slapping of hands.

Dad arrives home from work and assumes sick kid duty. He carries the slightly smashed cardboard box of popsicles, most of its contents consumed, into the living room. He brings a paper towel, not a bowl. A bold yet risky move.

"What flavor do you want?"

"Root beer."

He leaves and goes back into the kitchen. I hear Mom sigh in frustration.

"No root beer, Jean Bean."

"Grape."

"No more grape. Just cherry or orange."

"Oh man! Orange, I guess."

Dad carefully wraps the paper towel around the wooden stick and hands me the fluorescent orange obelisk.

The scene repeats itself the next day with a new box of assorted popsicles. My sister brings home my box of Valentines and homework from school. The sick sofa is getting crowded. It is my birthday. Dad arrives home from work with a plastic bag he whisks into the kitchen. I open my birthday gifts. Mom snaps photos to record the day. I play with Orange Blossom and Lemon Meringue—my two new Strawberry Shortcake character dolls.

Dad comes over to the sick sofa with a paper towel and a paper-wrapped popsicle.

"What flavor do you want, Pussycat?"

"Grape," I answer without looking up.

"Not root beer?"

"They don't have root beer. No store has root beer anymore." Defeat lingers on my lips as I put the hat back on Orange Blossom.

"This looks like root beer to me."

Doll hits the floor. I reach out for the paper towel-wrapped handle.

My dad tells me he found root beer popsicles at Wawa. Sold individually. Dad took every last frozen treat out of the freezer up to the counter.

The clerk said, "Whoa, someone likes root beer!"

"They're for my daughter. I've searched the town for these popsicles. My daughter is home with strep throat and it's her birthday and all she wants is root beer."

The wintergreen, anise, cinnamon flavors burst inside my mouth. ◆

South Indian Curry and Pomegranate Chicken

GRACE SEGRAN

Immediately after Raja's memorial service in London, I traveled with our daughter, Elizabeth, back to Berkeley, California, where she was in the final semester of her PhD program. Each day I forced myself to be useful and shopped at Trader Joe's downtown, walking the mile there and back. I cooked lunch and brought it to Elizabeth where she was working on her dissertation in UC Berkeley's Bancroft Library. We sat on a bench outside when the weather was fine and opened our lunch containers with various dishes and shared a meal the Asian way. Some days it would be Raja's mother's recipe of spicy South Indian lamb or fish curry and murdered vegetables. In our family and among Singaporean friends, vegetables cooked the Indian way were affectionately referred to as "murdered" because they were very soft, cooked to death, compared to my mother's Chinese stir-fries, which were done briskly and came out crunchy. Other days we would have stir-fried beef or prawns to go with crisp vegetables. The very dishes that we had shared with Raja.

"How's your thesis coming along?" I asked as I nonchalantly picked up the chili-covered, plump tiger prawn with my chopsticks and placed it on her noodles. It was a lovely winter's day, and we sat outside in our jackets sipping hot tea in between spoonfuls of Singaporean cuisine.

"Slow," she mumbled. "But getting there." She chewed pensively on the stem of the crunchy *kai lan* (Chinese kale) and swallowed. "How was your meeting at church this morning?"

"Fine. We are on the last chapter of Isaiah next week."

"Papa loved Isaiah. I remember he taught the sixty-six chapters over two years at our church in London."

"Hmm," I said wistfully, as I picked out a tiny piece of fibrous bark that had slipped into the wok. We ate in silence, ensconced in our own thoughts too painful to reveal, tending privately to our bleeding hearts.

In Berkeley, I knew no one. Safe from people who cared but offended with platitudes. *Oh be quiet*, I had wanted to say to them at the memorial reception. *Go away*. Berkeley was balm for my aching heart. It also afforded me a hiatus from decisions I knew I had to make. *Not just yet. Please.*

I attended Bible study and services regularly at the First Presbyterian Church four blocks from the apartment, even when I didn't feel like it. Some of the women who had lost their spouses reached out to me. They took me out to lunch and to Widows' Fellowship. They wanted to know what Raja was like, what he loved. They didn't tell me "he's in a better place" or "such is life."

I didn't know if I was going to make it through the loss by myself. So I checked in with the pastor. *Do you have counselors for grieving?* There was a widows' class that ran for eight weeks, but I had missed the cycle, and they assigned Merrilee, the coordinator of the program, to work with me personally.

We met several times at La Méditerannée, a Lebanese restaurant on College Avenue near the apartment. We always had the same thing—Merrilee's favorite dish, which also became mine—pomegranate chicken, drumsticks marinated in pomegranate sauce and baked with herbs, served with rice pilaf and sides of soup, hummus, and pita bread. The first time we met, I told Merrilee that I hated being referred to as "the widow" by friends and bureaucratic documents. *I'm Raja's wife. I'm still married to him; it's just that he's not here.* During our times together, she informally walked me through the steps of recovery, but I think what really helped was the friendship, conversation, Turkish mint tea, and pomegranate chicken.

When my ninety-day U.S. tourist visa came to an end, I returned home to London. Raja's shoes met me at the door. Just as he'd left them before he was taken to the hospital. A hollow echo reverberated through the house as I shut the front door. Berkeley felt like a dream. An ambrosial but ephemeral dream. ◆

Raisins

ROBERT BOUCHERON

Leaving aside the troublesome question of genetic engineering implied by seedless fruit, raisins are a healthy, all-natural snack to foist on children. Adults, too! Shake a few in the palm of your hand, and clap the hand to your open mouth, as though you heard a morsel of shocking news. Raisins are sun-dried grapes!

Sweet and chewy, raisins contain mostly sugar—fructose and glucose. No evil sucrose, so a diabetic person can indulge, within reason. Raisins are fat-free, gluten-free, and cholesterol-free. They contain no preservatives, chemicals, emulsifiers, artificial colors, or petroleum distillates. They have a little fiber, and minerals such as copper, iron, and potassium. When it comes to empty calories, you could do worse. Munch away!

Raisins come in flavors. There is the golden sultana, the tart red currant, and the exotic black Corinthian. The one you know best is the wrinkled brown speck, the ugly bug. Who said food always has to be pretty?

Add raisins to bland and unpalatable foods like oatmeal, bran muffins, and hominy grits. Their dark, fruity taste provides a much-needed accent. And don't forget texture! If you really aim to please, add cinnamon and nutmeg.

Storage is a snap. After you open the box, put the raisins in a plastic bag that zips, a bin with a cover that seals, or a glass jar with a rubber ring in a heavy lid that clamps. Refrigerate, or store in a cool pantry or a cellar, so long as the cellar is dry. If the cellar is gloomy, or the stair is steep, or you quail at the prospect of going down there, send a naughty child who deserves to be punished.

Raisins will retain their flavor, color, and nutritive value up to two years. They will keep even longer if frozen, and frozen raisins thaw quickly at room temperature. Still, if you have not used the raisins for over two years, why did you buy them in the first place?

At the back of the cupboard, while searching for something else, you may happen on a box of raisins for which you are not responsible, a brand you never heard of. Waste not, want not. On closer inspection, you may find the product has hardened into a brick the size and shape of the box. The sugar crystallizes, and the raisins turn to candy. To de-clump, use a spoon or a spatula to pry the raisins apart. Or pick at them with your fingers, which will get sticky and gross.

To chop raisins, toss one cup raisins with one teaspoon oil, and rapidly cut with a French knife. Also called a chef's knife, this is a steel blade about eight inches long, straight, and slightly curved at the tip. Surely you have one of these.

To plump raisins, cover them with very hot tap water, and soak for two to five minutes. They will transform into purple globes, like aphids swollen with sap that you pick off tomatoes in the garden, or ticks engorged with blood that you find on the dog. Longer soaking will result in loss of flavor and nutritive value. Use an egg timer, a miniature hourglass, or a device that clicks like a bomb about to explode. Drain before using.

If the children have been good, reward them with a game of Snap Dragon. Sprinkle raisins in a shallow bowl filled with brandy, turn off the lights, and set the brandy ablaze. One at a time, pluck the raisins with bare fingers and try not to get burnt. The dragon is the flickering blue flame. ◆

The Day a Receptionist's Recipe Took the Cake

EVA M. SCHLESINGER

It started innocently enough with a lemon cake.

I had been visiting my family, and on the train back to Boston, I happened to glance beneath my seat and saw someone's abandoned day planner. When I got home, I sent it priority mail to the woman whose New York address was listed on the inside front cover.

Less than a week later, FedEx was on my doorstep with a large box that had a Beverly Hills bakery as its return address. Inside the box was a lemon cake—a thank-you gift from the woman.

I took one slice, for quality-control purposes, and because this woman can't live on lemon cake alone, I brought the rest to the small publishers' office where I worked as a receptionist. I put the cake on a plate in the kitchen with a note that said, "Free Lemon Cake, Donated by Eva." Then I returned to my desk.

I had been at my job almost a year. My coworkers seemed like such fascinating people. I was in awe of them. I wanted to be them, instead of merely the nameless, faceless, front-desk person who had to deal with their never-ending calls and towering piles of mail without saying anything. The most I got from them was, "You're not ditzy, like our previous receptionists."

The day I brought the cake, however, people swarmed to my desk.

"What a generous thing to do."

"Has anyone ever told you what a sweet person you are?"

I was thrilled. Everyone loved me. At last, I had potential as a coworker and a person.

Not long after, I felt inspired to do some baking. I had been a bread baker for my college co-op, and at one point in my life I enjoyed making a different kind of bread each week. So I consulted a bread book and made cranberry bread. A friend had told me sugar was bad for one's health. I resolved to use unsweetened cranberries and no sugar—I was opposed to baking with it.

I was also opposed to the bread's taste. I had a habit of not following directions, so when bread didn't turn out the way the book said, I'd make up my own recipe. I decided to reincarnate the failed bread as chocolate coconut cranberry cake. I used coconut milk that had been in the cupboard for three years, vanilla, almond butter, ginger, cinnamon, nutmeg, and five ounces of unsweetened cocoa. It took three hours to bake at 325 degrees. Periodically, I'd take it out of the oven, mash it up and rearrange it in the pan. It looked like a rich, black mound with peaks and valleys. It tasted like stale, mildewed cardboard. I couldn't bear to eat it, nor did I wish to throw it out. What a waste of good ingredients!

I brought the finished product to work. If my coworkers had loved me for the lemon cake, they would love me even more for my very own creation.

I put my cake on a plate in the kitchen with a note that said, "Free Chocolate Cake." Then I went to my desk and waited. Midafternoon, I saw that someone had taken a sliver. I cheered for that person.

Toward the end of the day, I overheard Crystal, the marketing manager, talking with Jason, an editor, by my desk while they sent faxes.

"Do you know who brought that cake?"

"What cake?"

"It's on your side of the office, and you don't know what I'm talking about? Someone took a piece and nearly gagged."

I felt sick to my stomach. I was no longer loved, no longer seen as worthy. I wondered if I should speak up. I'd only embarrass myself. I might get in trouble. What if I was fired?

I stayed quiet, as usual. Then I thought about how I had invented the recipe with my own creativity, and how happy the process made me.

In between my receptionist lines—"Hello, may I help you? Please hold while I transfer your call."—I leaned forward to my colleagues. "Are you talking about the chocolate cake in the kitchen?"

"Yes," Crystal said, "Do you know who made it?"

"I did."

Her mouth flew open. "I'm sorry if I hurt your feelings. I didn't even try your cake. It probably was very good."

I had wanted their approval, but I had my own. And that was the icing on the cake. ◆

Maize Madness

KATHRYN TAYLOR

Corn on the cob: **summer's** superstar. August is high season for corn in Pennsylvania. I never plan a vacation during August. I would miss my summer's quota of corn on the cob.

Maize madness. I inherited my condition. I was born into a family of corn on the cob lovers. When I was a little girl growing up in Hollidaysburg, PA, I would tag along with my mother to Baronner's farm market down on Juniata Street, just past Legion Memorial Park on the way to Duncansville. I remember wandering around bins of cantaloupe and watermelon, tabletops covered with peaches, plums, tomatoes, cucumbers, green beans. But my mother was there to buy corn. Four dozen ears of corn, usually twice a week. She was not preserving it for winter. Our family of seven (Mom, Dad, Pap-Pap, Jimmy, David, Beth, me) regularly ate that many ears of corn at any one sitting.

Four dozen ears of corn (at 25¢ a dozen) loaded into the back of the green station wagon. Four dozen ears of corn dumped outside the kitchen door for various family members to help husk. Four dozen ears of corn dropped for three minutes into cauldrons of boiling water on the electric stove in the kitchen and on the old gas stove down in the basement. Four dozen ears of corn piled high on platters carried into the dining room.

All seven of us loved corn, but Dad, Mom, and I most of all. Ear after ear dripping with butter, showered with salt, picked up with our fingers. No cute little plastic ears of corn with tiny steel spikes jabbed into the ends of the cob. No wussy corn holders for us. I ate typewriter-style, starting with the stem end to the left and working across, three rows at a time, *click, click, click, click, bing!* Then on to the next set of three rows. Stripped cobs would pile up on platters earlier relieved of the intact cobs. Of the four dozen ears, I could polish off a dozen all by myself. Of course, I didn't eat anything else for dinner. No hamburger. No barbequed chicken. No baked potato. Certainly nothing green. Maybe some sliced tomatoes on the side. Maybe an orange Creamsicle for dessert.

Downing a dozen was a feat I could still accomplish into my thirties. While those days are long gone and now I usually tuck into only two, my craving for fresh Pennsylvania farm corn has not diminished. No packages from the vegetable section of the freezer aisles in the Acme in winter will do. No ears shipped up from Florida in late spring, or even Maryland in June. I never order corn on the cob at a restaurant. Who knows where that corn has come from or how long it has been sitting in a steamy pot.

I have had to adapt to certain changes. At first glance my local farmers market still looks reassuringly similar to Baronner's (if considerably larger), with tables of tomatoes and deep counters of corn. But 25¢ a dozen? A quarter wouldn't even get you one full ear of corn. And the choices are no longer simple. It's not just yellow, white, or bicolored. Now there is a multitude of varieties, some with names that are beyond understanding. Yellow could be True Gold or Sundance. White could be Country Gentleman or Martian Jewels. Bicolored could be Sugar & Gold or Quickie. There's even a multicolor variety called Hookers. And that's just to name a few.

Yet I remain undaunted. I still buy corn two or three times a week through August.

September is soon enough for a vacation. ◆

The Empress of Ice Cream

PAMELA FELCHER

For most of my dad's young life, he lived above and worked at Felcher's, his parents' neighborhood candy store and lunch counter, tucked between P&G's Bar and Grill and Simpson's Hardware Store on Amsterdam Avenue, between 73rd and 74th Streets in Manhattan. Christopher Morley would watch my dad as a tiny boy play in front of that store, and immortalized him as "the man of the future" in his novel *Kitty Foyle.*

Throughout college and law school, my dad scooped ice cream and served sandwiches at the lunch counter while his then-girlfriend, my mother, perched herself on a stool out front, eating Fudgsicles, unwittingly enticing much of the passing parade, including several members of the 1950s New York Giants football team. I can still see the scoop my father kept from Felcher's—the well-worn wooden handle and scored thumb press that pushed the slim metal band that would release the perfect scoop, every time.

When I was a kid growing up in Riverdale, in the west Bronx, my dad would take us to Goldman's Luncheonette on Johnson Avenue, where I discovered the unbeatable combination of tuna on rye and chocolate malteds. That I could buy Archie Comics on the way out was another boon.

But once my dad moved back to the city, sadly without my mom, my sister, and me, I surprisingly discovered an ice cream that I did not like, an ice cream I believed to be one of the staples of divorced fathers everywhere: Häagen-Dazs Rum Raisin. All my pleasurable associations with ice cream could have been erased by the shifts in my home life, accompanied by that brief flavor lapse. Fortunately, my tastes are not as ephemeral as the treat itself.

During my teen years, Carvel and Dairy Queen both opened up in my neighborhood, Dairy Queen on Riverdale Avenue; Carvel on Johnson. I am not sure whether it was my loyalty to the long-gone Johnson Avenue Goldman's, but for me Carvel won that competition. I could not get enough of those Flying Saucers, soft-serve chocolate-dipped cones, and Tom Carvel's fanciful ice cream cakes (what an inspired combo that is, by the way, ice cream AND cake!).

Then came the ultimate revelation: Baskin-Robbins. I had heard about their ice cream for years. My grandma would return from a visit to my aunt in Ventura, California, who got through her pregnancies by practically living at her local Baskin-Robbins, with endless stories of Jamoca Almond Fudge.

Once those famed 31 Flavors landed in my neighborhood, sugar cones filled with two scoops of the coffee, fudgy, nutty ice cream had me scrambling for all the loose change I could muster. I'd like to say that Ben and Jerry's and Häagen-Dazs and McConnell's and Cold Stone are my other favorites, but I would be lying. My tastes are far too common. The Chocolate Cherry Overload that Breyer's has given us feels redemptive because of the large chunks of healthful cherry and dark chocolate, and Thrifty coffee ice cream—topped with Fox's U-Bet chocolate syrup, naturally—can perk up even the dullest day. And I think I may have gained all my winter weight the summer I discovered Trader Joe's Mint Chocolate Chip, filled with dark chocolate pieces, not really chips at all.

Each year in my English classrooms I offer the students Wallace Stevens' poem, where "The only emperor is the emperor of ice-cream," and I say what an empire it is! ◆

Motha Tond/Big Mouth

DANIEL ARISTI

Tyache tond itke mothe aahe ki tyache dole ani nak tithe kasha bastaat kun-ach thauk, or, "With such a big mouth it's amazing that his face can still fit in nose and eyes." Mom would often recite this alone while chopping okra or coriander, because Dad was stuck in "transmit," typically about office politics at the textile mill. She would listen quietly. After all, *bayko navryachi saavli aste*, "the wife is the shadow of the husband."

Mom said she had coined this adage sometime in 1962, only months into her arranged marriage to my much older father. She whispered it to herself one afternoon over lonely tea and *mathi* (a biscuit made from flour, water, and cumin seeds), after one of Dad's hour-long monologues. Immediately she put a hand to her mouth: what sort of wife was she? Shame, shame on her! She was expected to be dutiful and obedient, like Sita, the wife of Rama. She felt so guilty that she forgot her tea and started roasting eggplants to make his favorite *baingan bharta* like she thought Sita would have done.

A year later she dared share her formula with cousin Sunita, who was visiting from Pune. And Sunita just couldn't stop laughing! The same thing happened with auntie Vandana, and with auntie Deepika, too. Before the year was over the women of the family had adopted the *Motha Tond* mantra as their secret handshake. "Sad as circus, but *so* true," lamented Auntie Arju.

One monsoon day in 1983 the whole thing came out in the open, during dinner at a table of fresh *chapatis* and *dal*. After another diatribe over missed job promotions reverberated unchallenged for three-quarters of an hour, Mom had had it. (Two decades as an audience of one). She looked at Dad, and changed one word in her battle cry. "His mouth" suddenly became "*your* mouth." Hands shaking, her Punjabi blood boiling and, hanging there in midair, this little adjective with a mind of its own.

Dad, shell-shocked, said nothing. His Sita (who'd have thought it?) was actually Durga, the demon-killer, eight sword-wielding arms at the ready! He folded *The Hindu* and left for the temple. And a thick calm descended upon the House of Joshi that lasted thirty years.

By the late 1980s Mom's mantra had fallen into desuetude.

The last recorded instance of its use in public is dated 12 March 2002, Mom's sixtieth birthday, at the prompting of aunties Gauri and Fareena. Mom said it once again, inside her kitchen inner sanctum, against a background of hot *pav bhaji* (thick vegetable curry) and in one fast go:

Tyachetonditkemotheaahekityachedoleaninaktithekashabastaatkunachthauk!

This time mild laughter only. Things had changed. Dad, sitting in the living room, had been retrenched for years now, and was too old and deaf to hear much of anything anyway.

So, the whole thing felt a bit like leftovers gone off. ◆

Hands Off the Black Jack

LISA ROMEO

My Noni lived in a tenement apartment in gritty Paterson, New Jersey, where her grandchildren always found icebox cake in the fridge, root beer ice pops in the freezer, and in the treats drawer, a bag of Circus Peanuts—bright orange, banana-flavored, too-sweet hard marshmallows shaped like peanut shells.

By the time I was seven, diabetes had taken Noni's right leg and much of her joy in eating, so she no longer dug into the peanuts bag with me or ate the icebox cake she'd made. The day we took our weekly walk to the bakery to buy a bag of coffee cake crumbs for a nickel, and she didn't share them, was one of the saddest days in my little life.

One treat Noni could still indulge was her Black Jack gum, stored atop the kitchen hutch, off limits to all eight grandchildren, even her beloved youngest grandchild—me. I was the only kid allowed to detach her artificial leg and climb into her lap when she leaned out the window singing Italian songs with ladies across the alley.

Mostly, I never cared about the gum. Who wanted to chew something that made your teeth resemble charcoal and your tongue look like you'd been sucking on a black marker? But how I loved its pungent smell, its blue-and-white packaging. I'd stand on the kitchen step stool to sniff the sharp, anise-like aroma, fascinated that one candy—black licorice, a favorite—could be the flavor for *another* candy.

"Go get my gum," Noni occasionally commanded. Meaning, fetch the entire pack. Only Noni could extract a stick, slowly unwrap and slide it into her mouth, then smooth and fold the wrapper and slip it into her smock pocket.

One wintry Saturday, Noni and I had already made pizza and played check-ers. While she rested, I read aloud from a book about horses; she liked that because she couldn't read English. When we ran out of entertainment, she told me stories while I flicked the lock-and-release lever on her wooden leg.

Finally, bored, I remembered the gum, and asked to try it.

"You may no like," Noni said. "It'sa strong."

"But I love licorice. Please?"

A tiny smile flickered, and she motioned toward the hutch.

I balanced the stick solemnly on my tongue before letting it touch my teeth. It was everything I feared—chalky, strongly flavored, so like and *un*like black licorice—and all I hoped: bold and bitter, like how I imagined coffee and other forbidden adults-only foods must taste.

Noni died not long after. I asked for her thin, worn, old quilt and slept under it until leaving for college.

I forgot about Black Jack gum until last August.

Three miles from my comfortable suburban home—halfway to the site of Noni's old tenement, razed decades ago for a highway ramp—stands a shiny store bulging with kitchen gadgets, pillows, clocks, art, and containers of every sort. There's an eclectic food section too, featuring things like salted-kale-pumpkin-soy cookies, bacon-flavored grits mix, antioxidant Wisconsin cherry preserves—and offbeat vintage foods you'd think vanished long ago. Including Circus Peanuts and Black Jack gum.

Back home, I place the gum pack on my kitchen table, and though I can't see any neighbors, I suddenly want to fling open the window, lean out, and sing an old Italian song. Instead, I open my laptop and learn that Black Jack was the first flavored gum, the first in stick form, and has a long-standing reputation for calming acid reflux. Noni frequently complained of *agita*. I picture her pressing fingers against her chest while grimacing. Did those moments coincide with her asking for gum? I don't remember.

I leave the gum on the table, not sure whether I want to chew a piece or keep the pack unopened. Then I move on to my original task: filling the new container I bought with linens for my son's first dorm room. I had offered a few times to buy him a new quilt. But he wants the one he selected when we repainted his room in sixth grade; it feels slightly worn and I think it's a bit juvenile. I smooth my hand over it, close the lid.

Finally, I unwrap one stick of Black Jack and balance it on my tongue. I fold the wrapper and slide it in the pocket of my yoga pants. Then I tuck the pack behind a vase atop my dining room hutch. ◆

Striking a Chord or Four

AMANDA SOBEL

I'm not sure why I first made *pulusu*, a tamarind-based curry from Southeast India. I think I was looking for something else (culinarily), came across a recipe for egg *pulusu*, and decided to give it a try. I got lucky. What I tried, on a whim, had an incomparable blend of flavors and textures: unctuous, mellow onion rounded by the depth of ground coriander; a sharp bite from tamarind buoying dense hard-boiled egg; crisp, bright, fresh coriander; ginger; garlic but only in a whisper … it spoke to my taste buds somehow. I couldn't quite figure out how, but I was in love. To say it struck a chord with me would be an understatement. I became a *pulusu* fanatic, determined to learn to cook at least some of its many variations.

Chance encounters occasionally take off like that. This dish, though, seems to have an effect on everyone I know. Every time I've cooked *pulusu* for people who haven't tried it before, they've fallen for it as strongly and immediately as I did. The problem is that, as an American living in Massachusetts, far removed from Southeast India, I don't know what I'm doing. I learned to cook this dish by vacuuming—sucking up any and all information I could find about it. I was vacuuming in a vacuum. I didn't know anyone who could tell me if I was preparing *pulusu* correctly, or even what the dish is supposed to taste like. I'm as perfectionistic as I am American, and this troubled me.

Sanjay Thumma, self-titled Vahchef at VahRehVah.com, helped me understand *pulusu* as a base to which cooks add different ingredients (eggs or okra or taro or fish or eggplant or bottle gourd or potatoes, for example). I watched all of Chef Thumma's *pulusu*-related YouTube content, trying to understand the nuances of this base. I still don't know what I'm doing, but I think it's a bit like Pachelbel's *Canon in D.*

Do you like this piece? Does it get stuck in your head? Pachelbel's *Canon* draws a strong response from most listeners. Many fall in love with it, even the first time they hear it, even if they're not accustomed to hearing Western classical music. Even if they don't like Western classical music. The piece triggers deep emotions. It's the base—in this case, a ground base of eight notes that repeat throughout.

Canon in D, especially the ground base, draws strong emotions from musician-comedian Rob Paravonian. He hates it. As a cellist responsible for sustaining those eight notes—no others—through the piece, he grew bored, bored, bored with *Canon in D*'s simplicity and repetition. He laments, in his YouTube-available "Pachelbel Rant," not only the simple structure of the ground base but also its ever-presence in modern popular music. Paravonian grumps, but members of Australian comedy band The Axis of Awesome posit, in "IV Chord Song," that this is the base for success. Something about the progression of sound speaks to people, and not only in Pachelbel's *Canon*. Many American, British, and Australian hit songs have been, quite literally, based on the base in *Canon in D*. Master the first four chords of it and you'll write a hit song, claim the members of The Axis of Awesome.

It's worth noting that the hit songs use four chords, not necessarily the eight-note ground base. That gives me a great deal of hope. I still don't know if I'm making *pulusu* correctly. I'm possessed by a quasi-obsession with real and authentic things that makes me doubt my efforts. But if I take the four-chord-hit-song-from-eight-note-ground-base as an example, I only need to get about 50 percent of this dish right for it to be fabulous. That should strike a chord with perfectionists and food lovers everywhere. ◆

The Curd of Cheese

AMY BARNES

In one-fell-swoop-cross-country move from the Midwest to the South, I lost my childhood food favorites: German cabbage and ground beef-filled bierocks, steamed hamburger sandwiches, French potato pie, peanut butter Amish pie and, most egregious of all, the cheese curd. Simple, humble food. The South served up other regional delicacies: sweet tea, grits, and even a regional replacement cheese, pimento. I was heartbroken at that Mason–Dixon cheese-curdless line.

I am a reverse cheese snob. My cheese needs to come from cows. American cows with two purposes: become steak or make milk to make cheese. Gary Larson *The Far Side* cows in a field eating grass. Not goats. Not llamas. Not tofu. Not nut milk disguised as cheese. Not French froufrou cheese aged in a cottage for thirty years. I also don't like cheese that isn't beige or yellow. Pink wine cheese is just not natural and may come from drunk unicorns. Paying $20 for an artistically arranged plate of miniscule specks of "cheese" and cornichons (people even make pickles fancy) isn't appealing. No farmers market cheese created in someone's bathtub. If a cheese will melt over pasta or between two slices of bread, I'm in.

When cheese comes to shove (and I would shove for cheese), my favorite down-to-earth cheese is the most humble: the cheese curd. Cheese curds are the ugly cheese stepsister. For the uninitiated, the cheese curd is like cottage cheese turned cheese but bigger. Chewy. Squeaky. Lumpy. Bumpy. Available in standard yellow or white versions.

When I looked for cheese curds south of the Mason–Dixon, I was disappointed and got odd looks when my Midwesterner accent confused my Southern friends into thinking I was looking for cheese "turds." After a cheese-curdless search, I even considered paying exorbitant shipping costs.

I went to Trader Joe's like a cheese addict going to meet her dealer. Sadly, no cheese curds. The very helpful staff told me they couldn't get quality cheese curds because they are fragile. They don't travel well from the Midwest to the South. At least the staff knew what a cheese curd was.

I left disappointed with a Trader Joe's consolation prize: mini peanut butter cups. I was too sad to eat them in the parking lot. I went across the street to Whole Foods, to a heavenly light and angelic music directing me to the cheese aisle. My old friend was alive and well in Tennessee: local cheese curds. I ate them in the parking lot like a naughty child with a stolen bag of candy. I expected sensory overload but got just—cheese. There's nothing wrong with that, but I expected more. Like cheese nirvana in my mouth. I didn't know if it was a "loved it as a kid, hate it as an adult" things, or if Whole Foods had gotten some of the rejected-by-Trader Joe's not-quality cheese curds. I sat there with my sad, guilty, empty cheese bag and turned it over to find the cheese had been made within an hour of my childhood hometown and shipped halfway across the country. It was like a childhood friend had sent me a letter. I decided to keep looking for my elusive childhood cheese curds.

I tried fried cheese curds at Zaxby's. And then, I had a cheese serendipity. An epiphany. At Target. I know Target can tell from my purchases when I'm pregnant. From the quantity of sweatpants and cheese I buy, they probably think I'm always pregnant. The computer formulas got it right; there were cheese curds in the deli. The Target inventory robots read my mind and ordered me cheese curds. The label just said "cheese." I knew what it was: my childhood in a bag. For $2.99. On that glorious day, in the place that thinks I'm pregnant (or cheese-crazy), I found the seventies again. I found that Midwestern, fold-of-the-map childhood that I thought was gone forever. I paid for the half-eaten bag of cheese curds with a guilty smile and blamed it on my kids. Who weren't with me.

Cheese curds can do that. Cheese plates with mysterious cheese bits can't; they leave you hungry and wondering why you're on a date with a dude who likes cheese plates. The moral is you can take the Midwest out of a girl, but you can't take out the cheese curds. Unless you snatch them out of my Target cart. I wouldn't suggest doing that. Midwestern/Southern girls are strong from cheese curd calcium. ◆

The Best Rhubarb Pie You've Ever Eaten

CMARIE FUHRMAN

Pie and whiskey are a staple at every Montana table. Any decent café has at least five kinds of fruit pie in the cooler, every server worth her sauce has a flask in her purse.

"Warmed up with a little ice cream?" I'd ask Carl every afternoon when he would come into the Homestead in Three Forks. "Yup," he said, "and a little of that special juice in my coffee."

My sister had colic as a baby. "We just put a little whiskey in her bottle," my mom said, and when either of us began to teeth, a little whiskey on our gums to ease the pain.

My first memory is of sitting on my grandpa's knee eating rhubarb custard pie. He was eating it crust first. A bite for him, a bite for me. Sipping coffee from the saucer. By the time the sun set in the western Montana sky there was just one piece left.

He woke me early the next morning and we shared it. "You two will cut me more rhubarb," my grandma ordered, smiling.

I once drank so much whiskey at the Miles City Bucking Horse sale that I rode a trash can bareback into the Montana Bar, where the bartender set up two more shots. When those were emptied, my friend tipped the trash can and wheeled me back out onto the street.

Another time, I was drinking whiskey with my friend Melissa Ortiz at a bar near Bozeman, when a woman from Pennsylvania told us she hated only two things about Montana: Mexicans and Indians. It was the only bar fight we were in, together.

When I was seventeen my mom said it was time we had "the talk." I prepared myself to hear her say words I was convinced she did not know: penis, fondle, hard-on, ejaculate.

"Honey," she started, "if you want a decent husband, you'll need to learn to make pies."

Years later the title of my Match.com profile read: Makes the Best Rhubarb Custard Pie You Have Ever Eaten.

On a date with the man who would become my husband, we went to a birthday party. I brought a rhubarb custard pie. Curt, the celebrant, tested the crust with his fork. He peeled the layers apart, looked at Randy and said, "She's a keeper."

A white Montana girl once drank so much whiskey she grabbed my shoulder and said, "Why don't you fucking squaws leave the white guys alone."

The last time I drank whiskey, Randy was dead. "Terrible accident," the sheriff said over and over. I drank enough Scotch that night to pass out on our kitchen floor. To vomit and sleep in it.

Three years ago, my mom and I visited her hometown of Philipsburg, Montana. She wondered about the rhubarb in her mother's backyard. The source of so many pies. We got up early the next morning and drove to the old place.

The ranch buildings had been razed. The land sold. Nothing stood: no corrals, no barn, no more kitchen table with crystal sugar dish and warm pie covered by soft tea towel.

I worked the shovel and Mom held the black trash bag. "Dig fast," she said, keeping her eyes on the highway, her first crime in eighty years. We placed three crowns of Grandma Carey's rhubarb in the back of my white

Matrix. She took two of them to Colorado, one for my sister, one for herself. I planted mine in Idaho.

Grandma Carey's rhubarb lives on my deck in a planter my father built. I cleared the snow from it this morning, saw furled leaves like red fists punching through frozen soil.

As I was bent to my work, my partner, Caleb, stepped onto our deck and said, "You can finally pick it this year." I had waited the requisite one year after planting, and a second to make certain it took. "Maybe there'll be enough for a pie." Whisking the last bit of spring snow from the soil and rising to stand beside him with confidence that went beyond baking skills, past the bars and ranches of my memory to a kitchen table where the future sat as a brown girl with black braids on her grandpa's knee, I took his hand and said, "It'll be the best you have ever eaten." ◆

Recipes for Success

We asked a few of our *Flash Nonfiction Food* authors to share the recipes that inspired their culinary narratives herein. Their responses appear below. May they move you to even greater heights of imagination—or at least give you an idea of what to cook for dinner tonight.

My Family's Sausage Stuffing

BY TINA TOCCO

2 packages Jones sausage (remove skin)
1 medium onion (finely chopped)
2 cans chicken broth
½ stick butter
½ bag Arnold bread stuffing (herb)
1 bag Martin's Potatobred soft cubed stuffing [Yes, that's the correct spelling of Potatobred—it's a brand name.]
Water (optional)

In a medium skillet, break sausage into small pieces and brown slightly. Add chopped onion. Stir until onion is cooked.

In a small saucepan, combine broth and butter. Cook on low heat until butter is melted. In a large bowl, combine stuffing and broth mixture. When sausage and onion are cool, add to stuffing mixture. Mix thoroughly with hands or wooden spoon. If mixture is too dry, add water to moisten to desired consistency.

Stuff cavity of turkey or, if preferred, place stuffing in a baking dish. If using a baking dish, cover with foil and place in oven after removing turkey. While turkey is cooling, cook stuffing for twenty minutes, covered. Remove foil and cook an additional five to ten minutes.

Enjoy!

Pie, Mash, and Liquor

BY JO VARNISH

Jellied eels would be added to serve, and, per my Dad's wishes, the pie would be served upside down.

The pie

500 grams of minced beef
1½ tablespoons of plain flour
250 ml of beef stock.
350 grams of plain flour
200 grams of suet
½ teaspoon of salt
Water (at least 400ml)

Fry the beef for about five minutes, breaking up the mince, until it browns. Sprinkle 1½ tablespoons of flour over the mince and stir. Add the beef stock and bring to a boil. Simmer for fifteen to twenty minutes. Leave to cool.

Sieve 350 grams of flour into a large bowl and carefully mix in the suet using a knife. Mix in the water. Add as much water to the mixture as possible, while keeping it solid. Refrigerate for thirty minutes. Hold briefly under running cold water. This pastry needs to be as moist as possible while still allowing you to roll it out. Roll it out to about two to three millimeters in thickness. Keep a spray bottle of water handy to keep everything moist.

Preheat the oven to 375 degrees. Place a tablespoon of water in each pie dish. Line the bottom of the pie with the pastry and cut so it covers the rim. Fill the pies with the mince, about ¾ full. Brush the rim of the with water, and add pastry to the top; cut and seal. Bake for thirty to forty minutes.

The mash

Mashed potatoes with butter and black pepper

The liquor (parsley sauce)

1 oz butter
1 oz flour
½ pint chicken stock
4 tsp fresh parsley, finely chopped
Salt
Pepper

Melt the butter in a pan. Add the flour and cook gently for one minute. Gradually add the stock and bring to a boil while stirring. Add the parsley, and season to taste

Serve with pie, mash (and jellied eels if you're adventurous!)

Aloo Bodi Tama

BY ANUJA GHIMIRE

50g fermented bamboo shoots (*tama**), sliced
½ cup black eyed peas (*bodi*)
½ tsp ginger, finely grated
2 cloves of garlic, crushed
2 medium potatoes (*aloo*), chopped
2 medium tomatoes, chopped
1 small onion, chopped
Finely chopped cilantro for garnish
2 tbsp cooking oil
1 tsp turmeric
2 tsp ground cumin
2 tsp ground coriander
1 tsp chili flakes
Salt to taste
*can be found in Asian grocery stores

1. Soak black eyed peas overnight. Drain the water.
2. In a small pan, fry the bamboo shoots in ½ tbsp of oil. Add a pinch of turmeric. Set aside.

3. Turn stove on medium heat, pour rest of the oil into saucepan.

4. Once the oil is heated, fry the onion, ginger, and garlic until golden.

5. Add potatoes and black eyed peas and fry for two to three minutes.

6. Add the spices.

7. Add the tomatoes.

8. Add bamboo shoots. Mix well.

9. Add four cups of water. Cover, boil, and simmer until the potatoes and peas are tender. Keep stirring to mix well. Takes about thirty minutes in medium heat.

10. Add cilantro for garnish.

Banana Bread

BY CECILIA GIGLIOTTI

1¾ cup flour
¾ cup sugar
1 tsp baking soda
Salt
2 eggs
3 bananas, mashed
½ cup canola oil
¼ cup buttermilk
1 tsp vanilla extract
1 cup walnuts, chopped

Preheat oven to 325 degrees. Lightly grease a 9"x5" loaf pan. In a large bowl, combine flour, sugar, baking soda, and salt. In a separate bowl, combine remaining ingredients (except walnuts) and stir until blended. Add banana mixture and walnuts to flour mixture and stir only to moisten. Pour batter into pan. Bake 75-90 minutes until a toothpick inserted into the center of the loaf comes out clean. Let cool in pan 10 minutes, then turn out onto a wire rack.

Classic Peanut Butter and Mustard Sandwich

BY JOEL LONG

This Montana classic will be the delight of toddlers, teenagers, and you with its wonderful medley of sweet, tangy, and viscous. The toothiness of Wonder Bread will blend with the creamy peanut butter while the yellow mustard will awaken the tongue with its brilliant zest.

2 pieces of Wonder Bread
2 tablespoon of Jif peanut butter, creamy
3 teaspoons of French's mustard

Separate two pieces of bread so they can be joined symmetrically.

Spread the peanut butter in spiral patterns, being careful not to tear the delicate bread.

Apply the mustard evenly to the other slice of Wonder. Do not let the mustard pool.

Join the two slices, pressing lightly to leave delicate thumbprints on both sides of the sandwich.

Serve immediately. For a good wine pairing try the classic Montana favorite, Boone's Farm, or Mad Dog 20/20.

Enjoy.

Liver pate (butter style)

BY STEVEN GOFF

20 lbs of liver
1 clove of garlic
7 ea onion (julienned)
1 quart of bourbon
1 gal cream
6 lbs of butter
2 tbs. black pepper
1 ea thyme bunch (sachet so you can pull out before pureeing)
Salt to taste

Melt 3 lbs. of butter. Caramelize onions and garlic in the melted butter. Cook until butter browns a bit. Throw sachet in to sizzle. Deglaze with bourbon and reduce au sec. Add liver and cook until it gets a little color on exterior. Add cream and black pepper. Simmer liver until just cooked through. Purée the entire mix, adding 3 lbs. of butter. Pass through chinois. Season to taste, and set.

Rhubarb Custard Pie and No Fail Crust

BY CMARIE FUHRMAN

4 cups cut rhubarb
1.5 tbs. sugar
3 tbs. flour
3/5 t nutmeg
2 eggs

Crust

3 c flour
1 t salt
1.25 c shortening
1 well beaten egg
5T water
1T apple cider vinegar

Crust

Cut together flour, salt, and shortening. Add beaten egg to water and vinegar. Mix well. Add to crumble mixture.

Filling

Beat eggs. Add flour, nutmeg, and sugar. Add rhubarb last. Pour in unbaked pie shell. Dot with butter before adding top crust. Add top crust and pinch together. Lightly coat with whole cream and sugar.

Bake at 435 degrees for fifteen minutes, then lower to 350 degrees until pie is done.

Contributors

Kim Addonizio's latest books are a memoir, *Bukowski in a Sundress: Confessions from a Writing Life* (Penguin), and a poetry collection, *Mortal Trash* (W. W. Norton). Her story collection *The Palace of Illusions* appeared in 2015 from Counterpoint/Soft Skull. Her other books include two novels, two guides to writing poetry, and several award-winning books of poems. Addonizio is the recipient of a Guggenheim Fellowship, two National Endowment for the Arts grants, and other awards. She lives in Oakland, CA and is online at www.kimaddonizio.com.

Maureen Mancini Amaturo is a New York-based fashion and beauty writer and a contributing columnist for the *Rye Record*. She teaches creative writing, produces literary arts events for Manhattanville College, where she earned her MFA in Creative Writing, and leads the Sound Shore Writers Group, which she founded in 2007. Her personal essays, creative nonfiction, short stories, and humor pieces have been published by *Ovunque Siamo*, *Mothers Always Write*, *Bordighera Press*, *Boned*, and *Baseballbard.com*. Her poetic tribute to John Lennon was published by the Beatlefest organization. She's had articles and celebrity interviews published in local newspapers and online.

Jonathan Ammons is an essayist, travel writer, and journalist living in Asheville, North Carolina. He is editor-in-chief of *The Dirty Spoon* and host of *The Dirty Spoon Radio Hour*, as well as a contributor to *Salon*, *100 Days in Appalachia*, and the alt-weekly *Mountain Xpress*, with bylines at Gannett and McClatchy. Find his work at Dirty-Spoon.com or follow his exploits on Twitter or Instagram @jonathanammons.

S. Makai Andrews is a student at Ithaca College, born and raised in Los Angeles, California. She is currently furthering her studies in writing and psychology and coming to the conclusion that in order to write well, you have to live well. Her published work can be found in *The Claremont Review, The Mighty, Jackelope,* and *Crab Fat Magazine,* among others.

Daniel Aristi was born in Spain. He studied French Literature as an undergrad (French Lycée in San Sebastian). He now lives and writes in Switzerland, with his wife and two children, and a white cat. Daniel's work is forthcoming or has been recently featured in *Salt Hill, decomP, Temenos Journal,* and *The Main Street Rag.*

Amy Barnes has words at a variety of publications, including *The New Southern Fugitives, Parabola, McSweeney's, Detritus Online, Taco Bell Quarterly, Maria at Sampaguitas, Tiny Essays, Flash Fiction Magazine, Lucent Dreaming,* and *FlashBack Fiction.* She is a reader for CRAFT and *Narratively,* and associate creative nonfiction editor for *Barren Magazine.*

Rebecca Helm Beardsall works at Western Washington University. She received her MA in English from Lehigh University and her MFA from Western Washington University. She has more than twenty years' experience in freelance writing in the United States and abroad. Her poetry and essays have appeared in *Origyns, SWIMM, West Texas Review, Two Cities Review, The Schuylkill Valley Journal, Amaranth, Common Ground Review, Poetry NZ,* and *Rag Queen Periodical.* She wrote and co-edited three books, including *Philadelphia Reflections: Stories from the Delaware to the Schuylkill.* Find her at rebeccabeardsall.com.

Cynthia Belmont is professor of English at Northland College, an environmental liberal arts school on the South Shore of Lake Superior, where she teaches creative writing, literature, and gender studies. Her work has appeared in a range of journals, including *Poetry, Natural Bridge, Oyez Review, Terrain. org,* and *The Cream City Review.*

Cherise Benton is a food literacy educator and aspiring farmer in Northeast Ohio. Her photography and poetry have been published in *Car Bombs to Cookie Tables: The Youngstown Anthology.*

Robert Boucheron grew up in Syracuse and Schenectady, New York. He worked as an architect in New York City and Charlottesville, Virginia, where he has lived since 1987. His stories and essays on architecture and literature are in *Bellingham Review, Fiction International, London Journal of Fiction, New Haven Review,* and the *Saturday Evening Post.*

H. E. Casson is a Canadian writer and library technician. Their work has been published in *Room, Cricket, Fireweed, Today's Parent Toronto, Smart Moves,* and *Grey Borders,* among others. They are of the opinion that the pigeon is nature's greatest achievement.

Rita Ciresi is author of the novels *Bring Back My Body to Me, Pink Slip, Blue Italian,* and *Remind Me Again Why I Married You,* and three award-winning story collections: *Second Wife, Sometimes I Dream in Italian,* and *Mother Rocket.* She is professor of English at the University of South Florida and fiction editor of *2 Bridges Review.* Visit her website at www.ritaciresi.com.

Catharina Coenen is a first-generation German immigrant to the northwestern "chimney" of Pennsylvania, where she teaches college biology. Her creative work addresses trans-generational effects of war. Her essays have appeared or are forthcoming in *The American Scholar, The Southampton Review Online, Superstition Review,* and elsewhere.

Renée Cohen is a world traveler and freelance writer. Her personal essays, prose, and flash fiction have appeared in *Accenti Magazine, Prairie Fire, The Globe and Mail,* the *Montreal Gazette, Reader's Digest, Brilliant Flash Fiction, Zvona i Nari Croatia,* in numerous volumes of the Canadian Authors Association Anthologies, and elsewhere.

Elaine Crauder's fiction has appeared in *Scoundrel Time,* the *Running Wild Press Best of 2017: AWP Special Edition;* the *Running Wild Anthology of Short Stories,* vol. 1; *Cooweescoowe; Penumbra; The Boston Literary Magazine;* and *The Eastern Iowa Review.* Another story earned The Westmoreland Award. Ten of her short stories are finalists or semi-finalists in contests, including finalists in *Bellingham Review's* 2015 Tobias Wolff Award and in the Mark Twain House 2015 Royal Nonesuch Humor Contest. "Dinner at Five" is her first creative nonfiction piece.

Dallas Crow is a high school English teacher in Minnesota. His nonfiction has appeared in a number of publications, including *Marathon & Beyond*, *Minnesota English Journal*, *New Madrid*, *North Dakota Quarterly*, and *Weber—The Contemporary West*.

Elizabeth Danek's stories have been published in *Mid-American Review*, the *Los Angeles Times Magazine*, and *VoiceCatcher*, as well as performed for Liars' League PDX. She has taught high school and adult education in Los Angeles; Munich, Germany; and currently in Portland, Oregon, where she resides.

Thad DeVassie is the author of *This Side of Utopia* (forthcoming from Cervena Barva Press). His work has appeared in *Poetry East*, *New York Quarterly*, *North American Review*, *West Branch*, *NANO Fiction*, *PANK*, and *Flash: The International Short Story Magazine*, among others. A lifelong Ohioan, he is the founder of a brand messaging + storytelling studio in Columbus, and is the cofounder of JOY VENTURE, a podcast and platform for sharing stories of unlikely and risk-taking entrepreneurs.

Terri Elders, LCSW, a lifelong writer and editor, has contributed to over a hundred and thirty anthologies, including multiple editions of *Chicken Soup for the Soul*. She writes feature articles and travel pieces for regional, national, and international publications. After a quarter-century odyssey, including a decade overseas with the Peace Corps, five years ago she finally returned to her native California, where she lives not far from her beloved Pacific Ocean. She blogs at http://atouchoftarragon.blogspot.com.

Pamela Felcher has been teaching high school English for thirty-four years in public, private, and religious schools in the Los Angeles area. She also taught freshman writing classes at Loyola Marymount University in the LEAP program for dancers on their way to a bachelor of arts degree through St. Mary's College in Moraga, California. Pam has published two collections of essays, *Eat Write* and *Is it June Yet: The Musings of the Bemused*, and in her spare time, she takes several dance classes a week. Along with a pair of dogs and cats, she has two horses whom she lives for!

Kathryn Fitzpatrick is a recent graduate of Central Connecticut State University, where she received the Leslie Leeds Poetry Prize and the Barry Leeds Critical Essay Award. Her writing has been published by *Cleaver Magazine*, *Unbroken Journal*, *Out Magazine*, and others, and was called "brutally honest and not school appropriate," by her high school principal. She lives in Thomaston, Connecticut, where she's working on an essay collection about Thomaston, called *Raggie*.

Sherrie Flick is the author of a novel and two short story collections. Her fiction is included in *Flash Fiction Forward*, *New Sudden Fiction*, and *New Micro*. Her nonfiction appears in *Ploughshares*, the *Wall Street Journal*, and *Creative Nonfiction*. She served as series editor for *The Best Small Fictions 2018* and is a submissions editor at *SmokeLong Quarterly*.

Lori Fontanes tells stories in various media about food, justice, technology, and the environment. She has raised vegetables, ducks, and a daughter in Westchester County, New York, where she has been a leader on conservation issues. Her work has appeared in *The Willowherb Review*, *Backyard Poultry*, *EcoWatch*, the Sundance Film Festival, and many other venues. She speaks about agriculture and ecology for organizations around the region and received her MFA in Creative Writing at Manhattanville College, where she is also an adjunct professor.

Sari Fordham teaches at La Sierra University. Her work has appeared in *Best of the Net*, *Passages North*, *Brevity*, *Green Mountains Review*, and *Isthmus Review*, among others. Her memoir, *Wait for God to Notice*, is forthcoming with Etruscan Press.

Kim Foster is a James Beard award-nominated and Folio award-winning food writer. You can read more of her essays at www.Kim-Foster.com and her micro essays on IG @KimFosterNYC.

Though **Tonno Bisaccio** current resides in a nation known for its vowels, history, lovely cars, and proper pizza, he was born and raised in Cleveland, Ohio. His writing can be found in *Alimentum*, *Apeiron*, *The Blue Nib*, and other places. He does, in any case, enjoy both raclette and the mountains.

CMarie Fuhrman is the author of *Camped Beneath the Dam*: *Poems* (Floodgate 2020), and co-editor of *Native Voices* (Tupelo 2019). She has published poetry and nonfiction in journals including *High Desert Journal, Yellow Medicine Review, Cutthroat, Whitefish Review, Broadsided Press, Taos Journal of Poetry and Art,* as well as several anthologies. CMarie is the 2019 recipient of the Grace Paley Fellowship at Under the Volcano in Tepotzlán, Mexico, a 2019 graduate of the University of Idaho's MFA program, a regular columnist for the *Inlander,* and an editorial team member for Broadsided Press and Transmotion. CMarie resides in the mountains of west-central Idaho.

Tamara Gane is a freelance writer in Seattle. Here work has appeared in *The Washington Post, HuffPost, The Independent,* NPR's *The Salt, Fodor's Travel,* and more.

Anuja Ghimire is from Kathmandu, Nepal. A Pushcart and *Best of the Net* nominee, her work found home in *Glass: A Journal of Poetry, The Brown Orient, The Good Men Project,* and *EcoTheo Review,* among others. Her chapbook *Kathmandu* is forthcoming from The Unsolicited Press in 2020. She lives near Dallas with her husband and two children and works as a senior publisher for online test development.

John Gifford is a writer and photographer, and the author of seven books, including *Red Dirt Country* (University of Oklahoma Press, 2019), and *Pecan America* (University Press of Kansas, 2019). He lives in Oklahoma. www. johngifford.net

Cecilia Gigliotti is an expatriate poet/essayist/scholar writing mostly in English and occasionally in Italian. Her recent publications include a poem in the anthology *Visiting Bob: Poems Inspired by the Life and Work of Bob Dylan*; an article in the collection *The Handmaid's Tale: Teaching Dystopia, Feminism, and Resistance Across Disciplines and Borders*; and an academic thesis entitled, "Looking Through a Glass Onion: John Lennon, Lewis Carroll, and a Literary Intersection for the Ages." She holds a Master of Arts in English literature from Central Connecticut State University, although she is far from mastering anything.

Steven Goff is the co-owner and executive chef of AUX Bar as well as Brinehaus Meat and Provisions, an Asheville-based food truck, and co-owner/co-chef of the Blind Pig Supper Club. Goff is responsible for day-to-day management of operations, menu design, business development, and cooking classes. Goff's work has been mentioned in *Food and Wine, Bon Appétit, Garden and Gun*, as well as many local publications. Goff lives in Asheville, North Carolina, with his wonderful wife and business partner Samantha Goff, their bevy of animals, and his daughter Emma Goff.

Diane Goodman is the author of three collections of short stories: *Party Girls, The Plated Heart*, and *The Genius of Hunger*. She lives in Phoenix, Arizona, where she is a professor of English at Grand Canyon University.

Allegra Grant is a chef with a thirst for adventure and passion for sustainability. Not only does Allegra love to cook, she enjoys the details and thrill of event planning. In winter of 2016 she moved back to her hometown of Atlanta for her next adventure as the culinary events manager for a national culinary tour visiting 20-plus cities. After hopping around on the rock-and-roll tour of heritage pigs she worked as a culinary project manager for Gumbo Marketing. Allegra recently started her own private chef and events business, Fenomenom LLC, in Wilmington, North Carolina, where she currently resides.

Mark Greenside is the author of *I saw a man hit his wife*, a collection of love stories; *The Night at the End of the Tunnel, or Isaiah Can You See?*, a dystopian novella; and two memoir/travelogues about living in France, *I'll Never Be French (no matter what I do)* and *(not quite) Mastering the Art of French Living*.

Shahnaz Habib has published her writing in *Creative Nonfiction, Agni, Brevity*, the *Guardian*, the *New Yorker* online, etc. She is the translator of *Jasmine Days*, originally written in Malayalam. Shahnaz teaches writing at The New School and at Bay Path University, and freelances for the United Nations.

Lisa Ohlen Harris works for a small-town dental practice in northwest Oregon. Her side hustle is adjunct teaching in Southern New Hampshire University's online masters program in English and Creative Writing. She's the author of *The Fifth Season: A Daughter-in-Law's Memoir of Caregiving* and *Through the Veil*, a memoir-in-essays of the years she lived in the Middle East.

Tom Hazuka has published three novels, over sixty-five short stories, and two books of nonfiction, both cowritten with C. J. Jones (*A Method to March Madness: An Insider's Look at the Final Four* and *A Summer That Can Change Your Life: A History of the Educational Opportunity Program at Central Connecticut State University*). He has edited or co-edited nine anthologies, including *Flash Fiction, Flash Fiction Funny, Flash Nonfiction Funny, Sudden Flash Youth,* and *You Have Time for This.* He teaches fiction writing at Central Connecticut State University. Links to his writing and original songs can be found at tomhazuka.com.

Sheila S. Hudson is a prize-winning author who has published fifteen cozy mysteries to date, three nonfiction volumes, and hundreds of articles, interviews, humor essays, and travel columns. She has been a member of Southeastern Writers Association since 1993 and served in many capacities, including as president. Her books *Bright Ideas to Make Your Writing Sparkle, Murder in the Classic Center* series, *Classic City Murders, Ministry Can Be Murder* series, *Silent Partner* series, *The Thursday Club, 13 Decisions That Will Change Your Life,* and *13 Decisions That Will Transform Your Marriage,* are all available on Amazon.com.

Claire Ibarra received her masters in Creative Writing from Florida International University. Her fiction, nonfiction, and poetry have been published in many literary journals and anthologies. Most recently, her work has appeared in *Fiolet and Wing: An Anthology of Domestic Fabulist Poetry, Embark Literary Journal,* and *Twisted Vine.* Claire's poetry chapbook, *Vortex of Our Affections,* was published by Finishing Line Press in 2017. She lives and teaches in Colorado; www.claireibarra.com.

Lakshmi Iyer is an alumna of the Yale Writers' Workshop. She has a certificate in creative writing from Simon Fraser University. Her work has appeared in *The Huffington Post, Mutha Magazine, Centered, The Verve, Chicago Now, Adoptive Families,* and *Women's Web.* Her family is the subject of a documentary on transracial adoption currently in production (@ourdaughters-doc). She blogs at www.lgiyer.com and is active on Twitter @lakshgiri.

Enid Kassner is a graduate of the Johns Hopkins University writing program. Her work has appeared in *Atticus Review*, *(b)OINK*, *Crab Orchard Review*, *Inscape*, *Watershed Review*, and other publications. She was awarded first place in creative nonfiction by the Coastal Bend Wellness Foundation. Enid writes and teaches yoga in Arlington, Virginia.

Robert King, aka "Food King," learned to eat in Astoria, Queens. He earned his PhD at the University of Utah and is on the Utah State University English faculty.

Jenny Klion's writing has appeared in the anthology *Flash Nonfiction Funny* (Woodhall Press, 2018), as well as in *Food52*, *Edible Long Island*, *Ploughshares*, *Longreads*, *The Rumpus*, *Tonic*, *Prevention*, *The Hairpin*, and more. She has worked in restaurant kitchens around the country, has a hundred-hour baking/pastry certificate, and was the proud owner of the now-defunct Sunday morning donation-only bakery experiment, Bakery 44, New York City.

Louise Krug is an assistant professor of English at Washburn University. She is the author of two memoirs about brain surgeries that she had in her twenties, *Louise: Amended* (one of *Publishers Weekly's* Best 20 books of 2012), and *Tilted: The Post Brain-Surgery Journals*. She lives in Topeka, Kansas, with her family.

American-French-Israeli hybrid **Jennifer Lang** writes about home. Her essays have appeared in *The Baltimore Review*, *The New Haven Review*, *Under the Sun*, *Ascent*, and on *Brevity*'s and NPR's podcasts, among others. A Pushcart Prize and Best American Essays nominee, she earned an MFA from Vermont College of Fine Arts and serves as assistant editor for *Brevity*. She is founder of israelwriterstudio.com and tweeter @JenLangWrites. "Consonance of Akko" is an excerpt from a memoir-in-progress.

Richard LeBlond is a retired biologist living in North Carolina. His essays and photographs have appeared in many U.S. and international journals, including *Montreal Review*, *Redux*, *Compose*, *New Theory*, *Lowestoft Chronicle*, *Trampset*, and *Still Point Arts Quarterly*. His work has been nominated for *Best American Travel Writing* and *Best of the Net*.

Eric D. Lehman teaches creative writing at the University of Bridgeport and his work has been published in dozens of journals and magazines, from *Edible Nutmeg* to *Gastronomica*. He is the author of seventeen books, including *New England at 400*, *Shadows of Paris*, *A History of Connecticut Food*, and *Becoming Tom Thumb*. He lives in Connecticut with his wife, author Amy Nawrocki.

A former features editor, news reporter, and filmmaker, **Marilyn Levine** has worked for the past eighteen years on the teaching faculty of the Massachusetts Institute of Technology's Comparative Media Studies/Writing Department. Her award-winning films, *Life, Death & Baseball* (1996) and *Something to Do with the Wall* (1991), have been distributed nationally and internationally. Ms. Levine, whose son, Adrian, died in 2016 following an accidental fentanyl overdose, is currently at work on a book about the opioid epidemic, the worst public health crisis in American history. She is also in production as librettist on an opera, *When Night Comes*, on the same topic.

Mark Lewandowski is the author of the story collection *Halibut Rodeo*. His essays and stories have appeared in many literary journals, and have received multiple Pushcart and *Best of the Net* nominations, as well as "Notable" listings in *Best American Essays*, *Best American Travel Writing*, and *Best American Nonrequired Writing*. He has taught English as a Peace Corps volunteer in Poland, and as a Fulbright Scholar in Lithuania. Currently, he is a professor of English at Indiana State University.

Joel Long's book *Winged Insects* won the White Pine Press Poetry Prize. *Lessons in Disappearance* (2012) and *Knowing Time by Light* (2010) were published by Blaine Creek Press. His chapbooks, *Chopin's Preludes* and *Saffron Beneath Every Frost*, were published by Elik Press. His poems and essays have appeared in *Gettysburg Review*, *Sports Literate*, *Prairie Schooner*, *Bellingham Review*, *Rhino*, *Bitter Oleander*, *Massachusetts Review*, *Terrain*, and *Water-Stone Review*, among others. He lives in Salt Lake City.

Alice Lowe reads and writes about life and literature, food and family. Recent essays have appeared in *Ascent*, *Bloom*, *Concho River Review*, *Hobart*, *Superstition Review*, and *Waccamaw Review*. Her work has been cited in

Best American Essays and has been nominated for Pushcart Prizes and *Best of the Net*. Alice is the author of numerous essays and reviews on Virginia Woolf's life and work, including two monographs published by Cecil Woolf Publishers in London. Alice lives in San Diego, California; read her work at www.aliceloweblogs.wordpress.com.

Mira Martin-Parker earned an MA in philosophy and an MFA in creative writing at San Francisco State University. Her work has appeared in various publications, including the *Istanbul Literary Review*, *North Dakota Quarterly*, *Mythium*, and *Zyzzyva*. Her collection of short stories, *The Carpet Merchant's Daughter*, won the 2013 *Five [Quarterly]* e-chapbook competition.

Cris Mazza's new novel, *Yet to Come*, is from BlazeVox Books. In 2017 Mazza's *Charlatan: New and Selected Stories,* chronicling twenty years of short-fiction publications, was released. Mazza has seventeen other titles of fiction and literary nonfiction, including *Something Wrong with Her*, a real-time memoir; her first novel *How to Leave a Country*, which won the PEN/ Nelson Algren Award for book-length fiction; and the critically acclaimed *Is It Sexual Harassment Yet?* She is a native of Southern California and is a professor in, and director of, the Program for Writers at the University of Illinois, Chicago.

Anne McGouran's nonfiction appears in *Global Comment, Queen's Quarterly, CutBank, The Smart Set, Coachella Review, Journal of Wild Culture*, and is forthcoming in *Gargoyle Magazine* and *Switchgrass Review*. Her fiction appears in *Understorey Magazine, Emrys Journal, CommuterLit*, and *Mslexia*. Born in Toronto, she resides in Collingwood, Ontario, where she has developed a fascination with ice huts and orchard ladders.

Dinty W. Moore is co-editor with Tom Hazuka of *Flash Nonfiction Funny* (Woodhall Press, 2018.) In addition to dandelions, he grows garlic and edible nasturtium flowers.

Kristina Moriconi is a poet and essayist whose work has appeared in a variety of literary journals and magazines including *Brevity, Superstition Review, Lumina, Literary Mama, Ruminate*, and many others. Her work has been selected as a finalist in *terrain.org*'s 2017 Nonfiction Contest and *december*'s 2018 & 2019 Curt Johnson Prose Award in Nonfiction, and awarded honorable mention in *Juncture*'s 2018 Memoir Contest. Moriconi earned her MFA from the Rainier Writing Workshop in Tacoma, Washington. She lives in the Philadelphia area and teaches in the Creative Writing MFA Program at Rosemont College.

Amy Nawrocki is the author of six poetry collections, most recently *Mouth-brooders*, published by Homebound Publications. Her essay, *The Comet's Tail: A Memoir of No Memory*, was a finalist for the 2018 Foreword Review Indie Book Awards and won the Mind-Body-Spirit Award from Living Now Books. With her husband Eric D. Lehman, she wrote *A History of Connecticut Food*, *A History of Connecticut Wine*, and *Literary Connecticut*. They also write the column "Ark of Taste" for *Edible Nutmeg*. She is an associate professor of English at the University of Bridgeport and lives in Hamden, Connecticut.

Jeff Newberry's most recent book is *Cross Country* (WordTech, 2019), a collaboration with Justin Evans. His writing has appeared in many print and online journals, including *Brevity*, *The MacGuffin*, *North American Review*, and *Sweet*. The poetry editor of *Green Briar Review*, he lives in Georgia with his wife and two children. Find him online at www.jeffnewberry.com.

Hope Nisly is a librarian who lives in Reedley, California. Her essays and short stories have been published in *Mojave River Review*, *Esthetic Apostle*, *Fredericksburg Literary and Arts Review*, and *Journal of Mennonite Writing*, among others. Her short stories have aired on Valley Writers Read, a program that aired on a Fresno-based NPR affiliate radio station.

Elizabeth Noll is an editor at the University of Michigan. She earned an MFA in Creative Writing at the University of Minnesota. Her essay "The Emperor's Cut" appeared in the book *My Caesarean: Twenty-One Mothers on the C-Section Experience and After*. She lives in Ann Arbor with her husband and son and two cats: Bella and Groot.

Lydia Oxenham's college roommate gave her stories a score of 1.8 out of 10. She's been proving her wrong ever since. So Raquel, if you're reading this, please go to lydiaoxenham.com. Those pieces are at least a 3.6.

Hannah Paige is the author of the novels *Why We Don't Wave* and *30 Feet Strong*. She has been the editor of the online literary journal, *The River*, and her work has also been published in *WaterSoup* and *Adelaide Maga-zine*. A California native, she currently lives in Maine, where she attends the University of Maine, Farmington, earning a BFA in Creative Writing and a BA in History.

During the 1950s and '60s, **Christine Perkins** began composing adven-ture and horror stories acted out by neighborhood kids in her hometown of Manteca, California, to relieve everyone's boredom on long, hot, summer days in the San Joaquin Valley. She took a writing hiatus during high school and college and eventually became a high school English teacher, working for thirty-four years, retiring, and then moving on to teach group fitness and yoga. She loves cooking and gardening equally, and her husband Tom and daughters Maggie and Grace and granddaughter Olivia more. She lives in Berlin, Connecticut.

Sherry Poff enjoyed an idyllic childhood in the hills of West Virginia. She now lives and writes in and around Chattanooga, Tennessee. Sherry is a member of the Chattanooga Writers' Guild. Her stories and poems have appeared in various online and print publications, including *Muscadine Lines*, *Foliate Oak*, and the *Chicken Soup for the Soul* series.

Robert Pope has published a novel, *Jack's Universe*, as well as a collection of stories, *Private Acts*. He has also published many stories and personal essays in journals, including *The Kenyon Review*, *Alaska Quarterly Review*, and *Fiction International*, and anthologies, including the Pushcart Prize and *Dark Lane Anthology*.

Rebecca Potter teaches high school English and Philosophy in central Kentucky, where she lives with her husband, three sons, and two bulldogs. She has an MFA in Creative Writing from the Bluegrass Writers Studio at Eastern Kentucky University. Her current project is a book of narrative essays that focus on her experiences in the classroom as a student and a teacher.

Richard Robbins was raised in California and Montana but has lived continuously in Minnesota since 1984. He has published six books of poems, most recently *Body Turn to Rain: New & Selected Poems*, in 2017. He has received awards from the Loft Literary Center, the Minnesota State Arts Board, the National Endowment for the Arts, and the Poetry Society of America. From 1986–2014, Robbins directed the Good Thunder Reading Series at Minnesota State University Mankato, where he continues to direct the Creative Writing program.

Lisa Romeo is the author of the memoir *Starting with Goodbye* (University of Nevada Press, 2018). Her short works are listed as Notable in *Best American Essays* 2018 and 2016, and have appeared in the *New York Times*, *Brevity*, *Longreads*, *O, The Oprah Magazine*, and dozens of literary journals, newspapers, magazines, and websites. Lisa's essays are also included in many anthologies, including *Flash Nonfiction Funny*. She lives with her husband in northern New Jersey and has two grown sons. Find her at www.LisaRomeo. net.

Cathy Rose's fiction and creative nonfiction has appeared in *Your Impossible Voice*, *Fifth Wednesday Journal*, *Fourteen Hills*, *Santa Clara Review*, *Steel Toe Review*, *Deep South Magazine*, and elsewhere. She grew up in Williamsburg, Virginia, and now lives in San Francisco, California, where she writes and is a psychologist in private practice. She holds an MFA in creative writing from San Francisco State University.

For over twenty years, **Joan Saddler** has been cooking and teaching others to incorporate organic whole foods and unrefined ingredients into their daily eating. Her expertise with macrobiotic foods and principles are based on the teachings of Michio Kushi/the Kushi Institute in Becket, Massachusetts, and John Kozinski, also of Becket. Joan has personally found freedom from various minor illnesses and has successfully avoided the need for pharmaceuticals due to the macrobiotic way of eating and lifestyle practices.

Eva M. Schlesinger is a recipient of the *Literal Latte* Food Verse Award, and her work has been nominated for *Best of the Net*, as well as included in *Cooking with the Muse* (Tupelo Press, 2016). She is the author of *Remembering the Walker & Wheelchair: poems of grief and healing* (Finishing Line Press,

2008) and three dancing girl press titles, for which she designed the covers. Her lemon cake story placed second at the October 2018 San Francisco Moth GrandSLAM and also made the audience of 1,400 laugh nonstop.

Daryl Scroggins lives in Marfa, Texas. He has taught creative writing and literature at the University of Texas at Dallas, the University of North Texas, and the Writer's Garret, in Dallas. He is the author of *Winter Investments*, a collection of stories (Trilobite Press), and *This Is Not the Way We Came In*, a collection of flash fiction and a flash novel (Ravenna Press).

Grace Segran has been a journalist and editor for over twenty-five years. Her work has been published in *Forbes*, *INSEAD Knowledge*, *Singapore Management*, *Insights*, and others. She lived and worked in Asia and Europe for most of her life before settling down in Boston, Massachusetts, six years ago, where she discovered creative writing at GrubStreet. Her creative nonfiction essays have appeared in *Entropy*, *Pangyrus*, the *Common*, and elsewhere.

Amanda Sobel teaches at the MIT Writing and Communication Center in Cambridge, Massachusetts. Her background in historical linguistics and medieval-poetry translation keeps her testing the ability of words to cross boundaries of time, geography, and culture. A visual artist and avid gardener, she thinks and teaches about capturing nonverbal experiences in words. She writes about music, food, plants, prepositions, translation, transformation, self-awareness, and how each of these can influence our perceptions of the others.

Sheila Squillante is a writer living in Pittsburgh, where she directs the MFA program at Chatham University. She is the author of the poetry collection, *Beautiful Nerve*, as well as three chapbooks. Recent work has appeared in *Crab Orchard Review*, *Signal Mountain Review*, *Phoebe*, *Copper Nickel*, and elsewhere. She also serves as online editor for *Barrelhouse*.

Skaidrite Stelzer lives and writes in Toledo, Ohio, where she is an assistant professor in the English Department of the University of Toledo. A Pushcart Prize nominee, her work has appeared in *Fourth River*, *Eclipse*, *Glass*, *Baltimore Review*, *Flock*, *Storm Cellar*, *The Cape Rock*, and many other literary journals, as well as in a number of anthologies.

Catherine Stratton is a writer and filmmaker living in Hoboken, New Jersey. Her work will be included in the Fall 2019 print issues of the *Delmarva Review* and the *Tahoma Literary Review*. She plans to continue working on her craft until she takes her last breath.

Kathryn Taylor has been a banker, a teacher, and a university administrator. All she really wanted to do was be E. B. White. Her essays have appeared in *Purple Clover* and in various Philadelphia-area publications, online and in print, including the *Philadelphia Inquirer* and WHYY, Philadelphia's NPR affiliate. An editor of two nonfiction books, she also teaches writing workshops as part of Princeton University's "Princeton Writes" program. She lives with her husband and two cats near Philadelphia. You can find her book review blog, "A Month of Books," and her essays, published or otherwise, at kathryntaylorwrites.com.

A professor of English at Colorado State University, **Deborah Thompson** has published numerous articles of literary criticism and creative nonfiction. Some of her creative nonfiction credits include the *Bellevue Literary Review*, *Briar Cliff*, *CALYX*, *Creative Nonfiction*, *Fourth Genre*, *McSweeney's Internet Tendency*, the *Missouri Review*, *Kenyon Review Online*, *Passages North*, and *Upstreet*. She won the *Missouri Review*'s 2008 Jeffrey E. Smith Editor's Prize in creative nonfiction and the 2010 *Iowa Review* contest in the nonfiction category. The latter essay, "Mishti Kukur," was awarded a Pushcart Prize.

Tina Tocco's flash fiction has appeared in *New Ohio Review*, *Crab Creek Review*, *Roanoke Review*, *River Styx*, *Harpur Palate*, *Passages North*, *Potomac Review*, *Portland Review*, and other publications. A *New Stories from the Midwest* nominee, Tina has been published in multiple anthologies, including *Wild Dreams: The Best of Italian Americana* (2008) and *Best Small Fictions 2019*. She was a finalist in *CALYX*'s Flash Fiction Contest (2013) and an honorable mention in the *River Styx*'s Schlafly Beer Micro-Brew Micro-Fiction Contest (2015). Tina earned her MFA in creative writing from Manhattanville College, where she was editor-in-chief of *Inkwell*.

Leeanna T. Torres is a native daughter of the American Southwest, with deep Indo-Hispanic roots in New Mexico. She is an Aldo & Estela Leopold Writer-in-Residence Program alumna (2014), and her work has appeared in the

New Mexico Review, *Blue Mesa Review*, *Tupelo Press Quarterly*, *Eastern Iowa Review*, *Santa Fe Literary Review*, and the anthology *Natural Wonders* (Sowing Creek Press 2018).

Alison Townsend's newest book, *The Persistence of Rivers: An Essay on Moving Water*, won the 2016 Jeanne Leiby Award. She is also the author of two award-wining books of poetry, *The Blue Dress: Poems and Prose Poems* and *Persephone in America*, and two poetry chapbooks. Her writing has won a Pushcart Prize, the Crab Orchard Open Poetry Competition, a Wisconsin Literary Arts Grant, and many other awards. Her essays have appeared in *Chautauqua*, *Parabola*, the *Kenyon Review*, the *Southern Review*, *Zone 3*, among others, and have been listed as notable in *Best American Essays*. Professor emerita of English and Women's Studies at the University of Wisconsin, Whitewater, she lives in the farm country outside Madison.

Laynie Tzena is a writer, performer, and visual artist based in San Francisco. Selected publications include *Allegro*, *Ascent*, *Bayou*, *Event*, *Helicon Nine*, *The Lake*, *Rabbit*, *Sonora Review*, and *Zone 3*. Tzena received an Avery Hopwood Award in Poetry and a Creative Artist grant from the Michigan Council for the Arts. She has been a Cranbrook Fiction Scholar and featured performer at the Austin International Poetry Festival, the Marsh, the Monkey House, and on Michigan Public Radio.

Jo Varnish moved from England at twenty-four, and now lives outside New York City. Her short stories, creative nonfiction, and poetry have appeared in many journals and literary magazines, including *Okay Donkey*, *X-R-A-Y Literary Magazine*, *Brevity Blog*, and *Nine Muses Poetry*. Jo has been a writer in residence at L'Atelier Writers for the past two years, and is currently studying for her MFA. Jo's website is www.jovarnish.com and she can be found on Twitter as @jovarnish1.

Erin Renee Wahl's work has appeared or is forthcoming in *Dirty Chai*, *Spiral Orb*, *Cirque*, the *MacGuffin*, and others. She has two micro-chapbooks of poetry: *Secure the Night* (Bitterzoet Press) and *Cloud Physics* (Ghost City Press). Her work in many areas and genres can be found via a crafty Google search. She lives in New Mexico and works as a librarian.

A winner of the *River Styx* International Poetry Contest, runner-up for the Iowa Review Fiction Prize, and finalist for the Starcherone Prize, the DIAGRAM Innovative Fiction Prize, and the Paul Bowles Fiction Award, **Jesse Waters** is a recipient of a North Carolina Artist's Grant to attend the Vermont Studio Center, and is currently director of both the Bowers Writers House at Elizabethtown College and the West Chester University Poetry Center.

Brian Phillip Whalen's debut collection of fiction, *Semiotic Love [Stories]*, is forthcoming from Awst Press (2021). His work has appeared in the *Southern Review, Creative Nonfiction, North American Review, Sonora Review*, and elsewhere. Brian teaches at the University of Alabama.

Charlotte Whitty was born in New Orleans, Louisiana, where she was raised by her eccentric mother, an artist and devout Catholic. Charlotte, a staunch agnostic, currently lives in Louisville, Kentucky, and works as a real estate agent and ESL/citizenship instructor for elder refugees. She holds undergraduate degrees in French, cultural geography, and secondary education in French, and has had several personal essays published in *Elephant Journal*. She is a traveler who creates a spot of home wherever she lands. Charlotte's favorite people and greatest teachers are her three children, who have made a decent mother out of her.

Chris Wiewiora spent his childhood in Warsaw, Poland, where his parents served as evangelical missionaries behind the "Iron Curtain." He earned an MFA in Creative Writing and Environment at Iowa State University. His nonfiction has been anthologized in *Best Food Writing* and *Two-Countries: U.S. Daughters and Sons of Immigrant Parents*, as well as published in *Gastronomica* and on *Wanderlust*. He is the author of a travelogue memoir about growing up and going back to Warsaw, *The Distance Is More Than an Ocean* (Finishing Line Press, 2020). Read more at www.chriswiewiora.com.

Credits

Kim Addonizio: "Hardly Any Food at All" is reprinted by permission of the author.

Maureen Mancini Amaturo: "Breakfast Served Daily" was previously published in *Ovunque Siamo*, Vol. 3/Issue 5, July 1, 2019. Reprinted by permission of Maureen Mancini Amaturo.

Jonathan Ammons: "Only the Lonely" was previously published in *The Dirty Spoon*. Reprinted by permission of the author.

S. Makai Andrews: "Cook's Box—Vegan" is reprinted by permission of the author.

Daniel Aristi: *"Motha Tond/*Big Mouth" is reprinted by permission of the author.

Amy Barnes: "The Curd of Cheese" was previously published in a longer format in "The Dot" (on Medium) on August 28, 2018. Reprinted by permission of Amy Barnes.

Rebecca Beardsall: "Root Beer Popsicles and the Sick Sofa" is reprinted by permission of the author.

Cynthia Belmont: "Early Thanksgiving" is reprinted by permission of the author.

Cherise Benton: "Cookie Monster" is reprinted by permission of the author.

Tonno Bisaccio: "Raclette" is reprinted by permission of the author.

Robert Boucheron: "Raisins" is reprinted by permission of the author.

H. E. Casson: "All Ten Provinces and Both Territories" is reprinted by permission of H. E. Casson.

Rita Ciresi: "Hunger" was previously published in *Storm Cellar*, August 2017. Reprinted by permission of Rita Ciresi.

Catharina Coenen: "Oranges" is reprinted by permission of the author.

Renée Cohen: "Kuidaore: A Taste of Japan" is reprinted by permission of the author.

Elaine Crauder: "Dinner at Five" is reprinted by permission of the author.

Dallas Crow: "Blood Oranges" originally appeared in *100 Word Story*. Reprinted by permission of Dallas Crow.

Elizabeth Danek: "Translations" is reprinted by permission of the author.

Thad DeVassie: "Holy Bread" was previously published in *PANK* (Issue 4.02). Reprinted by permission of Thad DeVassie.

Terri Elders: "Proof of the Pudding" is reprinted by permission of the author.

Pamela Felcher: "The Empress of Ice Cream" is reprinted by permission of the author.

Kathryn Fitzpatrick: "Scab Eaters Anonymous" is reprinted by permission of the author.

Sherrie Flick: "Learning" was previously published in *American West Airlines Magazine* 13.2 (1998): 56. Reprinted by permission of Sherrie Flick.

Lori Fontanes: "Something Fishy" is reprinted by permission of the author.

Sari Fordham: "Arrival" is reprinted by permission of the author.

Kim Foster: "Fear Cooking" is reprinted by permission of the author.

CMarie Fuhrman: "The Best Rhubarb Pie You've Ever Eaten" is reprinted by permission of the author.

Tamara Gane: "How to Be Poor" was originally published in *The Journal of Compressed Creative Arts* in March 2019. Republished by permission of the author.

Anuja Ghimire: "Potatoes, Peas, and No, Please" is reprinted by permission of the author.

John Gifford: "For the Love of Pie" was first published in the *Christian Science Monitor* as "Pie Transports Me" on April 18, 2013. Reprinted by permission of John Gifford.

Cecilia Gigliotti: "Bananas" is reprinted by permission of the author.

Steven Goff: "Enough Is Enough" was previously published in *The Dirty Spoon*. Reprinted by permission of the author.

Diane Goodman: "Lunches with Louie" is reprinted by permission of the author.

Allegra Grant: "Friday Service" was previously published in *The Dirty Spoon.* Reprinted by permission of the author.

Mark Greenside: "I Cooked This for You" was previously published in *(not quite) Mastering the Art of French Living*, copyright by Mark Greenside, reprinted by permission of Skyhorse Publishing.

Shahnaz Habib: "Hospitality" was previously published in *Brevity.* Reprinted by permission of the author.

Lisa Ohlen Harris: "Comfort Food" was previously published in *Brevity* and in *The Fifth Season: A Daughter-in-Law's Memoir of Caregiving*, Texas Tech University Press, 2013. Reprinted by permission of Lisa Ohlen Harris.

Tom Hazuka: "Foie Gras or Faux Pas?" is reprinted by permission of the author.

Sheila Hudson: "Two Sides of the Same Buffet" is reprinted by permission of the author.

Claire Ibarra: "Things Left Behind" was previously published in *Real: Pure Slush*, vol. 3, 2012. Reprinted by permission of Claire Ibarra.

Lakshmi Iyer: "Of Samosas Fresh and Stale" was previously published in *The Dirty Spoon* blog. Reprinted by permission of Lakshmi Iyer.

Enid Kassner: "Tiny Florets" is reprinted by permission of the author.

Robert King: "Food Evolution: From the Mountains to the Mississippi" is reprinted by permission of the author.

Jenny Klion: "Mayonnaise and Apricot Jam" was previously published in *Groknation*. Reprinted by permission of Jenny Klion.

Louise Krug: "That's What We Said: Public Versus Private Eating" is reprinted by permission of the author.

Jennifer Lang: "Consonance of Akko" is reprinted by permission of the author.

Richard LeBlond: "Eating America" is reprinted by permission of the author.

Eric D. Lehman: "Buffalo Gourmet" is reprinted by permission of the author.

Sarah Wesley Lemire: "You've Been Chopped" was previously published in *Hartford Magazine*.

Marilyn Levine: "Kitchen Dalliances" is reprinted by permission of the author.

Mark Lewandoski: "Dinner for One" is reprinted by permission of the author.

Joel Long: "Peanut Butter and Mustard Sandwiches" is reprinted by permission of the author.

Alice Lowe: "B Is for Breakfast" was previously published online in *Hobart* literary journal, March 31, 2019. Reprinted by permission of Alice Lowe.

Kristina Moriconi: "Stalemate" is reprinted by permission of the author.

Mira Martin-Parker: "The Thanksgiving Bird" was previously published in *Gravel*, Fall 2017. Reprinted by permission of the author.

Cris Mazza: "Feeding Time" was previously published in *Brevity*. Republished by permission of the author.

Anne McGouran: "Ma'amouls and Nuns' Bellies" is reprinted by permission of the author.

Dinty W. Moore: "Weed Eaters" is reprinted by permission of the author.

Kristina Moriconi: "Stalemate" is reprinted by permission of the author.

Amy Nawrocki: "Go Ahead, Break Me" is reprinted by permission of the author.

Jeff Newberry: "Butchering" was previously published in *Brevity*. Reprinted by permission of Jeff Newberry.

Hope Nisly: "Death by Corn Candy" is reprinted by permission of the author.

Elizabeth Noll: "Black Pearl" is reprinted by permission of the author.

Lydia Oxenham: "True Grits" is reprinted by permission of the author.

Hannah Paige: "A Blonde, A Brunette" is reprinted by permission of the author.

Christine Perkins-Hazuka: "Edible Gifts" is reprinted by permission of the author.

Sherry Poff: "Making Sherry Eat" was previously published in *Chicken Soup for the Soul, Food and Love,* copyright 2011 by Chicken Soup for the Soul Publishing. Reprinted by permission of Sherry Poff.

Robert Pope: "Fire and Pie" was previously published in *Remembered Arts Journal,* Fall 2018. Reprinted by permission of Robert Pope.

Rebecca Potter: "How to Make Mamaw's Biscuits" is reprinted by permission of the author.

Richard Robbins: "Driving William Stafford" was previously published in *Brevity*, Issue 30, May 2009. Reprinted by permission of the author.

Lisa Romeo: "Hands Off the Black Jack" was previously published on The Inquisitive Eater, https://inquisitiveeater.com/2018/12/08/hands-off-the-black-jack-by-lisa-romeo. Reprinted by permission of the author.

Cathy Rose: "Maynard, Now Gone" was previously published in different form in *Deep South Magazine*, July 2015. Reprinted by permission of Cathy Rose.

Joan Saddler: "Food Fight" is reprinted by permission of the author.

Eva M. Schlesinger: "The Day a Receptionist's Recipe Took the Cake" was previously published in the *San Francisco Chronicle*, May 24, 2019. Reprinted by permission of the *San Francisco Chronicle.*

Daryl Scroggins: "A Meal in Venice" is reprinted by permission of the author.

Grace Segran: "South Indian Curry and Pomegranate Chicken" is reprinted by permission of the author.

Amanda Sobel: "Striking a Chord or Four" is reprinted by permission of the author.

Sheila Squillante: "Four Menus" was originally published in *Brevity*, Issue 25. Reprinted by permission of the author.

Skaidrite Stelzer: "Kidney Stew in the Summer of Love" is reprinted by permission of the author.

Catherine Stratton: "We Ate When We Were Hungry" is reprinted by permission of the author.

Kathryn Taylor: "Maize Madness" was previously published in a modified version in *The Swarthmorean*, Aug. 16, 2019 issue. Reprinted by permission of Kathryn Taylor.

Tina Tocco: "The Sausage Stuffing" was previously published in *Italian Americana*, November 2007. Reprinted by permission of Tina Tocco.

Leeanna T. Torres: "Tortillas" is reprinted by permission of the author.

Alison Townsend: "Valentine" was previously published in *Brevity*, issue 45, January 18, 2014. Reprinted by permission of the author.

Laynie Tzena: "Betty Crocker's Unwritten Rules" originally appeared on the blog "Love at First Bite," www.cookwithlaynie.blogspot.com (Sept. 2009).

Jo Varnish: "When Food Becomes Love" is reprinted by permission of the author.

Erin Renee Wahl: "Tortilla Chips" is reprinted by permission of the author.

Jesse Waters: "Fast Food" was previously published in *Brevity*. Republished by permission of the author.

Brian Phillip Whalen: "Dear Erik" was previously published in different form as "Teufelsdröckh, Give Up the Ghost" in the *Southern Review* (Volume 53, Issue 2, 2017). Reprinted by permission of Brian Phillip Whalen.

Charlotte Whitty: "Finding Home" is reprinted by permission of the author.

Chris Wiewiora: "Warsaw Market" is reprinted by permission of the author.